Elemental
Magic

"Who wouldn't want a whole system to perform serious magic all summed up in one book? *Elemental Magic: Traditional Practices for Working with the Energies of the Natural World* by Nigel Pennick delivers exactly that. Furthermore, it details how to work in harmony with the world around us—something that we all instinctively know is becoming more and more important with every passing decade."

IAN READ, ENGLISH EDITOR OF *CHAOS INTERNATIONAL* AND *RÛNA* MAGAZINES

"Nigel Pennick's *Elemental Magic* is a pithy primer on the ancient yet eternally relevant ways of engaging with the hidden workings of the ensouled world that surrounds us. This accessible little manual of hard-won wisdom offers basic instruction in an array of European folk-magic practices, along with a plainly worded overview of the enchanting folklore and enchanted worldview that underpins these hallowed customs. Ornamented with finely wrought images by the author himself, in his concomitant role as a spiritual artist and craftsman, the end result is more than a modest handbook—it is a *quintessential* one, in the best archaic sense of the word."

MICHAEL MOYNIHAN, PH.D., COEDITOR OF *TYR: MYTH—CULTURE—TRADITION*

"*Elemental Magic* serves as a toolbox of knowledge and techniques to further a person's understanding of the natural world around them. Written in a manner that allows the work to be incorporated by a variety of occult fields, Pennick offers both practical and philosophical means of ingress into this wide reaching arena. A worthy addition to any library."

DANIEL YATES, OCCULT PHOTOGRAPHER
AND AUTHOR OF *ARCANUM*

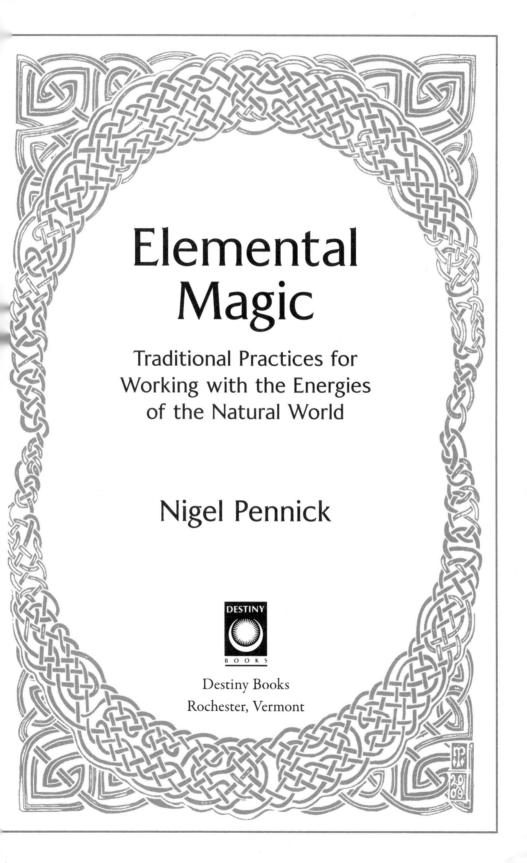

Elemental Magic

Traditional Practices for Working with the Energies of the Natural World

Nigel Pennick

Destiny Books
Rochester, Vermont

Destiny Books
One Park Street
Rochester, Vermont 05767
www.DestinyBooks.com

Text stock is SFI certified

Destiny Books is a division of Inner Traditions International

First edition published in the United Kingdom in 2001 by Thorsons under the title
Natural Magic
Second edition published in the United Kingdom in 2005 by Lear Books
First U.S. edition published in 2020 by Destiny Books

Cataloging-in-Publication Data for this title is available from the Library of Congress

ISBN 978-1-62055-758-7 (print)
ISBN 978-1-62055-759-4 (ebook)

Printed and bound in the United States by Lake Book Manufacturing, Inc.
The text stock is SFI certified. The Sustainable Forestry Initiative® program
promotes sustainable forest management.

10 9 8 7 6 5 4 3 2 1

Text design by Priscilla H. Baker and layout by Virginia Scott Bowman
This book was typeset in Garamond Premier Pro and Trenda with Majesty and
American Uncial used as display typefaces

To send correspondence to the author of this book, mail a first-class letter to the
author c/o Inner Traditions • Bear & Company, One Park Street, Rochester, VT
05767, and we will forward the communication.

Contents

The Natural Power in All Things

This book is about the practical techniques of traditional spirituality known as natural magic. Traditional spirituality seeks to achieve harmony between the world of human activities and that of nature. It does not preach human dominance over nature, neither does it seek to disempower human activities. To be in balance with the world is to be neither its master nor its victim.

The down-to-earth practical spiritual techniques of natural magic straddle the boundaries between the subtle, inner world of the mind and spirit, the material outer world, and the otherworldly. Magic comes about through interaction between the inner experiences of the human spirit and the outer experiences of the physical world, both natural and human-made.

Magic has often been defined as being the art of making changes come about according to the human will. If we take this definition, then almost every act of human creativity (and destructivity) can be called magical. Indeed, much of human technological civilization today would appear magical to our ancestors if, by some act of magic, they could be brought back to life.

Magic is often presented as a means of bringing something into existence out of nothing. The magician waves a magic wand, and—hey presto!—the thing desired appears from nowhere. That, of course, is stage magic, which is not magic at all, but the creation of illusions by human ingenuity. However, that is not the magic of this book. Because of this difference, some ceremonial magicians and witches spell the word *magic* in a pseudoarchaic way: *magick*. But when I refer to magic in this book, I am describing something else. Natural magic is essentially a spiritual, not a material, technology. It does not deal with gods and goddesses, spirits and demons. It is the power of everyday objects and human actions. Its power comes directly from nature, the natural forces of the four elements and the processes of existence.

Essentially, magic works on a nonmaterial level. It is an inner process that can be developed by means of certain well-defined spiritual techniques. Its primary aim is not the alteration of outer factors, though this is important. It is primarily aimed at the spiritual empowerment and development of the individual. These techniques are described in this book.

Like any human invention, magic can be used altruistically, for the good of others, or selfishly, without regard for others. Traditional spirituality recognizes that all things are interconnected and that we cannot be selfish without doing harm to others. Natural magic follows traditional spirituality, which seeks to be in harmony with all around us. To practice natural magic does not require us to renounce our family or religion. Neither does natural magic criticize or desecrate traditional holy symbols or objects. We venerate them as aspects of the universal divine principle, just as we expect our own symbols and objects to be respected by others.

Natural magic brings out the natural power in all things. It is a fundamental principle that we should never use this power for personal gain. We should not use it to subvert the free will of others or to coerce or manipulate other people or entities, even in times of conflict. Practitioners of natural magic should wish nothing and no one ill. Natural magic is not an end in itself. It is a means of upholding our free will and directing it toward personal growth. It is a way that we can seek to live according to eternal spiritual values.

NIGEL CAMPBELL PENNICK

1

Mother Earth

"The Earth is not an inanimate body, but is inhabited by the spirit which is its life and its soul. All created things draw their strength from the Earth Spirit. This spirit is life; it is nourished by the stars and gives nourishment to all living things that it shelters in her womb." So wrote the medieval European alchemist Basilius Valentinus.

We humans are part of the planet Earth; our bodies are made of the matter of Earth, and the conditions on Earth are perfect to sustain human and other life. It is natural, then, to view Earth as the mother of us all, the giver of life to all living beings. As human beings, we are part of all life, for life on Earth is one indivisible continuum. It is only when we feel one with the primal roots of existence that we experience wholeness.

Traditional spirituality, of which natural magic is a part, teaches us that we are not separate from nature and have no special privileges. The planet Earth, the plants, and the animals have as much right to exist as we do. It is not proper for human beings to wantonly destroy nature: like other creatures, we may take only what we need to live our lives in harmony, health, and beauty. To perform natural magic, we must always bear this in mind. Natural magic is the right usage of the creative force that exists within all things, including us. This creative force is neutral. It has no direction until it is directed by a conscious will. So it is up to us to direct it for the good of all beings, without subverting the free will of others.

BASIC STRUCTURES

The aim of natural spirituality is to live well, whatever we do. Being in harmony with nature does not mean that we should passively accept those natural processes that tend to destroy us. It means recognizing the underlying laws and patterns of nature and using them wisely. We can live harmoniously only when we follow the true principles of nature. These true principles are the basic ways that existence operates, and by understanding and following them, life can be made easier.

The principle of the law of the unity of opposites is one of the most significant themes in natural magic. It tells us that there can be no existence without nonbeing; there can be no life without death,

Fig. 1.1. The Wheel of the Year

no creation without destruction, no beginning without an end. Every aspect of everything is important; we can do nothing at all that will not have some effect, however small, on ourselves and the world around us. European traditional spirituality emphasizes this oneness of humans with the world: we must be aware of the possible outcome of every action we take and try our best to do no harm to the world or to other sentient beings.

Existence has a natural process that has a threefold or triadic structure: start—process—finish; otherwise, beginning—middle—end. This appears in life as the threefold phenomenon of birth, life, and death. Throughout their philosophy, the ancient Celtic bards recognized this threefold structure of being. This is expressed in the ancient writings called *The Triads of Britain,* in which the wisdom of the bards and Druids is taught in threefold sayings.

TIME AND THE SEASONS

Certain parts of the world have distinct seasons that come in regular cycles each year. These cycles have affected the development of culture, religion, and magic. The seasons dealt with in this book are those of the temperate Northern Hemisphere areas, covering Europe, Asia, and North America. The cycle of natural magic follows the cycle of the year. This exists because of the form of the Earth and its orbit around the sun. The year is divided naturally into two halves, which are further subdivided into four quarters. The two halves are the dark and light halves of the year. In the dark half, the nights are longer than the days. In the light half, the days are longer than the nights. At the transition points between the two halves are the equinoxes, when day and night are of equal duration. At the spring equinox (in late March), the light half begins, and at the autumnal equinox (in late September), the dark half.

The quarters of the year are defined in relation to the solstices, or turning points of the sun. From the summer solstice, the middle of the light half of the year (in late June), the length of daylight each day steadily declines and the length of the night increases. At the middle of the dark half of the year is the winter solstice (in late December). After the winter solstice, the longest night of the year passes, and the length of daylight each day increases. This increase continues through the spring equinox, when both day and night are of equal length, and the light half of the year is entered. The proportion of light to darkness continues to increase until we are back at the summer solstice again, when daylight is at its maximum and the night is the shortest.

The interrelationship of light and dark in the twenty-four-hour cycle of the day is essentially the same as the cycle of the year, having the same fourfold structure. But, except at the equinoxes, the relative length of the quarters is not equal. Whether we find it in the light/dark cycles of the day, the year, or the moon, this is a natural principle that underlies the existence of many beings and things. Because of this, certain seasons are more magically appropriate for certain activities than are others. Activities to do with birth, growth, and renewal are best performed in springtime, while those of endings, death, and dissolution are best done at the beginning of winter. Similarly, certain activities are best conducted at sunrise, noon, sunset, or midnight.

In addition to the cycle of the sun through the year, there is the lunar cycle. This is independent of the sun, and in any one solar year, there are thirteen full moons. The moon's cycle takes just longer than twenty-eight days, and it is divided, like the year, into two halves and four quarters. At the new moon, the moon is invisible from Earth, being illuminated by the sun on the opposite side. It is in complete darkness, as far as we are concerned. Then comes the first thin crescent, gradually waxing, until, a week later, it is the half-moon or first quarter.

The moon continues to grow, by now having more lightness than darkness, until it is full. The full moon is the time of total light. Now the moon begins to wane, and, a week later, it is in its last quarter, again a half-moon, facing in the opposite direction. Here, the moon enters the dark half of her cycle. Finally, waning further, she disappears at the next

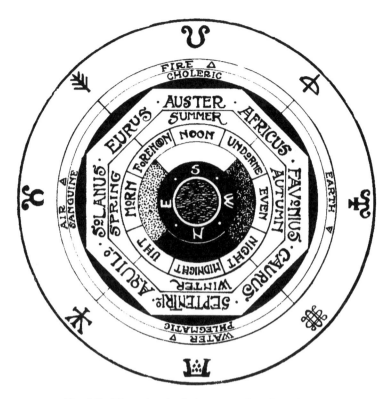

Fig. 1.2. The wheel of the year, the directions,
times of day, elements, and humors

new moon. In former times, it was thought that the moon in each cycle was indeed a new one. The moon's cycle is essentially the same as the cycle of the day and the year.

Natural spirituality has no place for artificial festivals and celebrations in the calendar. These are invariably the record of some historical event (real or imagined) that supporters claim has changed the world in some way. All religions, political systems, and nation-states have these days, whether to commemorate the birth of a prophet or hero, a revolution, or the foundation of the state. These are subjective, often support human power structures, and ultimately depend on the accuracy of calendars to maintain their true position in the year. Even the months and dates are part of this unnatural worldview.

The equinoxes and the solstices and the phases of the moon, on the other hand, are real events, as are the birth of the first lamb of the year, the appearance of the first leaves of springtime, and the harvest. They are natural times, independent of human ideology or belief. When we conduct our activities by the calendar, then we are using a human-made system that may not be in harmony with the natural flux of the seasons and the weather. For example, springtime may come early or late in the year, but it is not defined by a date on a calendar that says "First Day of Spring." We know when it is springtime by the blossoms and the new leaves on the trees. If the leaves have not yet appeared, even when the calendar tells us spring has begun, we know then that it has not *in reality*. When we perform our magic according to these natural happenings, then we are truly in harmony with nature.

CYCLES OF TIME

Natural magic understands time to go in cycles. I have mentioned the cycles of the sun and the moon, which define the day and the year. There are other earthly cycles that determine the qualities of time. One is the vegetation cycle, which follows the actual conditions of seasonal temperatures. These lag behind the sun because the Earth heats up slowly in the light half of the year and cools slowly in the dark half. The vegetation year is divided into two parts, the *Flower Year* and the *Harvest Year*. The Flower Year is a cycle whose low point is November–December and whose high point is May–June, while the Harvest Year has its low point in February–March and its high point in August–September.

Unlike the year that follows the progress of the sun, the Flower and Harvest Years vary greatly from year to year, according to the progress of the seasons. These vegetation years are the origin of the most ancient traditional festivals, which mark the four most important points within them. Today, when these festivals are observed,

Fig. 1.3. The Magic Light

they are linked to the sun calendar, as dates. But in former times, they were celebrated when the signs of nature showed people that it was time. They are known today by their old Scots and Irish Celtic names, but they are observed more widely than in just the Celtic countries of northwestern Europe.

The Harvest Year begins with the festival of lights, known by the two Celtic names of *Imbolc* and *Brigantia*. This is the low point of plants, in the depths of wintertime. The next festival of the vegetation year is *Beltane,* when the Whitethorn tree (or May tree) blossoms and the young leaves are flourishing on the trees. This is usually

Fig. 1.4. Samhain

celebrated on May 1 in the solar calendar, but, traditionally, Beltane is when the May tree blossoms, and not before. This is the high point of the Flower Year.

The third festival is *Lammas,* otherwise called *Lughnasadh* (pronounced *Loo-na-sa*). This is celebrated when the first loaf of bread from the wheat or barley harvest is made. It, too, is linked with the solar calendar and is celebrated on August 1. The fourth festival is *Samhain* (pronounced *Sow-ain*). This is also linked to the solar calendar, being celebrated on November 1. The Harvest Year ends here, for Samhain is the "third harvest." The first harvest is Lammas, when the grain is harvested. The second is at the autumnal equinox, when the fruits are harvested, while the third is at Samhain, the traditional time to slaughter animals to preserve their meat for the coming winter (see fig. 1.4).

THE DAYS OF THE WEEK

The days are measured by a seven-day cycle, and each day has a name. Each of the days of the week is aligned with a specific planetary power, sometimes personified as a goddess or god. These weekdays are used all over the world, no matter what religion or calendar is in force. Magically, they are significant, for they have individual and distinct powers. In English, their names recall the ancient goddesses and gods of the Anglo-Saxons. Tuesday is named after the god of law and order, Tîw. Wednesday recalls the god of knowledge, Wôden (see fig. 1.5). Thursday is named after Thunor, god of thunder, and Friday after the goddess of love and sexuality, Freia. Saturday is dedicated to the Roman god of aging and time, Saturn.

Although the sevenfold cycle of weekdays goes on in a neverending sequence, Sunday is taken as the first day of the week. As its name tells us, Sunday is the day dedicated to the sun. It is a good day for creative energies, self-reliance, and reinvigorating the vital spirit. Its corresponding color is gold. Monday honors the moon. Its power

Fig. 1.5. Wôden

is not the best for beginning the working week, being representative of the impressionable, sensitive, and withdrawn inner elements of the human psyche. Its color is silver. Tuesday commemorates the red planet, Mars, bringing energy, assertiveness, and endurance.

Wednesday is dedicated to the planet Mercury. It is a good day for activities connected with the intellect and human communication. Its color is sky blue or violet. Thursday is the day of Jupiter, associated with profoundly uplifting spiritual powers. Its color is purple. Friday is dedicated to the Morning and Evening Star, the planet Venus. It is a day of beautiful cooperation in human activities, though some consider it unlucky to start a new venture on a Friday. Friday's color is pale blue. Saturday is the day of Saturn. Its powers tend toward the materialistic side of existence, bringing heaviness and limitations. Its color is gray or black.

THE FOUR ELEMENTS

Natural processes are the basis of all existence. Nothing is sustainable for any length of time that does not base itself on the true principles of nature. The traditional way of understanding the workings of nature symbolically is to see it through the four physical elements—fire, air, water, and earth. In northern regions, a fifth physical element, ice, is recognized. In addition to the four or five physical elements, another subtle element, that of spirit, is recognized. This is the quintessence, or *nwyvre,* a subtle, all-pervading spiritual element that pervades and empowers the physical elements.

Fire

Fire symbolizes the lightest things of existence, the energy and spirit. Its corresponding direction is south. There are five earthly manifestations of fire. Three are natural, and two are artificial. The primal fire of the Earth emerges from volcanoes. Fires are sometimes kindled by lightning, which is a heavenly manifestation of fire. Sometimes the internal heat of things makes them burst into flames through spontaneous combustion. These are the three natural forms of fire.

The two other forms of fire are produced by humans. They are struck fire, where a spark is made by striking flint and steel (or pyrite), and need fire, made through friction. In modern magical usage, struck fire is produced by lighters, while need fire comes from matches. In ancient times, fire was venerated as a goddess. In many holy places, there were sacred fires that were tended by priestesses and were never allowed to go out. They symbolized the eternal principle of fire in the universe.

Air

Air is the element whose magical direction is the east. Scientifically, it is composed of around one-fifth oxygen and four-fifths nitrogen, with some other inert gases and human-made pollutants. When we breathe, we take in oxygen, which most creatures on Earth need to exist. The air is literally our life's breath, and because of this, it is important magically. I discuss the nature of breath in the human being in chapter 5, "The Power Within."

Traditionally the air is considered to be ruled by the air elementals, which include zephyrs, sylphs, dragons, and gremlins. Most importantly, the winds are personified, bearing names that characterize their qualities. These vary from place to place, depending on the local qualities of the winds. Each location gives them their own local names, and there are traditional sayings, rhymes, and songs that describe their qualities. The qualities of the individual winds differ from place to place, according to landscape and climate, so it is not possible to list them here.

Traditional magicians have always been in demand to call up the wind, and there are certain techniques that are still taught today. Whistling up the wind is the simplest. Facing toward the direction from which the wind is wanted, the practitioner whistles in a certain way, concentrating on the increase of the breath. Offerings in stones con-

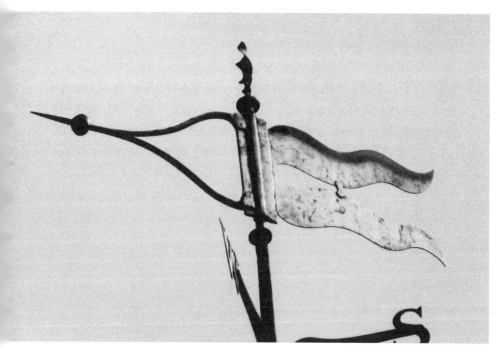

Fig. 1.6. Weather vane on Christ's College in Cambridge

taining natural depressions are also a traditional means of wind raising. The offerings, such as milk, ale, or grain, are laid in the hollow in the direction from which the wind is needed. The hollowed surface is an inverted reflection of the dome of the heavens, and the correspondence is clear. Until sails were replaced by power units, fishermen in the Baltic Sea constructed stone labyrinths on rocky islands and danced through them to call up favorable winds.

Good air and bad air are both significant magically. A place can have either a good or a bad atmosphere—literally, that which we breathe in—physically, psychologically, and spiritually. Places with bad air can bring disease or disharmony, and there are traditional magical ways of altering the qualities of the air to bring about psychic changes. This is called *laid air*. The air is known to have different spiritual qualities at different times of day, too. People also put on "airs and graces" when they step out of their true ways of behaving.

Water

Water is heavy and flowing; it circulates. Its direction is the west. Like the other elements, it is symbolized and personified by an array of sprites, including neckans, undines, urisks, water-horses, kelpies, nixies, the Lady of the Lake, the Kraken, mermen, and mermaids. These express various states of water: in static pools, flowing streams and rivers, whirlpools and waterfalls, waterspouts and tides. Each river has its own spirit, god, or goddess, and many river names reflect this. To us as air-breathing beings, water manifests the law of the unity of opposites. Without water, our life cannot exist, but water can also kill us, by drowning.

Earth

Earth is the lowest element, the basis of all. Aspects of this element are dealt with in the next chapter, chapter 2, "Mineral Magic," and chapter 6, "The Magic of the Land."

Ice

Ice is counted as an element in the Northern Tradition, the spiritual tradition of central and northern Europe. It is not ever-present, as are the other four elements, but it exists permanently in the polar regions and on high mountains and is a seasonal element in many places. The solid, static form of water, ice symbolizes massive and unavoidable processes. Its elemental spirits are the ice giants, vast, slow, and enormously powerful, like glaciers and icebergs. Ice ranges from the delicate, flowery sixfold patterns of snowflakes to the continent-wide icecap of the Antarctic and the icy planetary surfaces of the moons of Jupiter and Saturn.

The Quintessence

The final element is different from all the others in that it is not material. It is the quintessence, the subtle spiritual empowerment of the physical elements. As such, it is described as a universal cosmic breath, without which there would be no physical existence. It appears as a kind of primal energy, connecting and relating to everything that exists. This primal energy exists everywhere, and that includes within us. Human awareness and consciousness are empowered by this element. It can be directed by human desire and willpower to any part of the body and also projected outside it. Magic is the harmonious control and management of this power. In itself, this element has a neutral character. It can pick up surrounding influences and be a medium for them. It is patterned and colored by the psychic atmosphere of places and people and can be affected by human activities.

PSYCHIC ENCLOSURES AND SACRED SPACE

Natural magic deals with the subtle and unseen energies and powers of our environment. Through attunement with the primal roots of being, natural magic gives us the means to do something positive with our lives. Essentially, it is a human way of managing the spiritual essence of our existence. The spiritual essences that we need for this may or may not be present in the natural qualities of a place, and so we frequently need to create them. When we empower objects, meditate, or conduct self-empowering ceremonies, we usually need to create a psychic enclosure. Collect together everything you need before starting. You will not be able to leave the enclosure once it has been set up without destroying it. Ideally, it should be in a place where you are not likely to be disturbed by curious or interfering people.

The first thing to do is to make a borderline around the place where you will work. This should enclose an area large enough to contain yourself, any other participants, and all of the things you need. The shape of the enclosure is less important, but a circle or a square is the easiest to manage. To empower the borderline, walk around it nine times in a sunwise (clockwise) direction. It is best to be ceremonially dressed and to carry a power object, such as a stave or wand. As you walk, visualize a line of blue light following you and laying itself down on the boundary line. Once this ninefold circuit is finished, stay within the boundary. Next, empower the four directions with appropriate amulets. To the north, corresponding with the element of earth, put a stone. To the east, for air, burn herbs as incense. In the south, for the element of fire, light a candle; and in the west, for water, place a wooden bowl of fresh water.

The boundary and elements are now in place, creating the sacred space. Now purify this sacred space with the water of empowerment. This is ceremonially empowered salt water. It is best to use seawater taken with the incoming tide. Charge the water with protective energy by visualizing a stream of vibrant blue-white light entering the water from your hand. As you visualize the empowerment, chant a spell such as:

> *Into this water*
> *I direct my might and main,*
> *That it will be pure and clean,*
> *In the service of the elements.*

When you cannot get seawater, then a strong mineral water will do. If seawater or mineral water is not available, then freshwater from a river, lake, or well can have sea salt added to it, with the spell:

> *Here is salt,*
> *Salt is life,*
> *To clean this place,*
> *Free from strife.*

Under no circumstances should tap water be used, as it has been chemically treated, making it useless magically. Sprinkle the water of empowerment sunwise around the boundary and then in a spiral toward the center of the sacred space. Again, visualize a trail of blue-white light following the sprinkled water. The place is now ready for use, set aside magically from the rest of the world.

2

Mineral Magic

ELEMENTAL FORCES: EARTH

Of the four elements, the mineral kingdom comes under earth. Poetically, the rocks, which give the landscape its form, are called "the bones of the earth." Symbolically, stone stands for the static, blocking principle of immobility. But although stone appears to us to be eternal, even the hardest of materials are worn away by the processes of time. On the seashore, over vast periods of time, the sea rounds off chunks of rock to become pebbles, breaks them, and, little by little, reduces them to tiny grains of sand. But on the human timescale, we cannot see this taking place, but can only see the process in our mind's eye.

The Spiritual Nature of the Mineral Kingdom

Traditional spirituality teaches that the mineral kingdom is not lifeless matter but has its own spiritual nature. Each stone, gem, crystal, and metal has its own spiritual nature, which can interact with the human spirit. When we alter, modify, or destroy pieces of the mineral kingdom, we affect the spiritual nature of the world. This understanding, almost absent from modern technological civilization, is at the root of the arts of the alchemists. Twentieth-century alchemists believed that physicists, in "splitting the atom," have subverted the spiritual evolution of the mineral kingdom.

There are many kinds of stones, crystals, gems, and metals in the mineral kingdom, and it is not possible to list them all here. I give only the more notable or significant examples of each, as encountered most frequently in natural magic. Others that you may come across will also have their own potential value in appropriate applications.

Natural Magic Stones

Holeystones or hagstones are stones with a natural hole that passes right through from side to side. It is the hole that gives the holeystone its virtue, not the kind of stone. These are stones whose solid material has been penetrated by the grinding effect of smaller stones and sand in flowing rivers or by the tides of the sea. They are stones of protection, being hung up in barns, stables, garages, and houses. It is best to hang holeystones by a cord of natural material, such as flax, hemp, or leather. Chains of holeystones, in nines or multiples of nine, are particularly pleasing both aesthetically and magically.

Amber is a fossil resin sometimes used as incense, taken as a medicine, or worn as jewelry or amulets. Before the fall of Communism, the valued clear yellow amber from Eastern Europe was rare and expensive. Now amber from Poland and the Baltic countries has become readily available in the West and is worn for its beauty and for its healing qualities, for it is a promoter of bodily energy.

Fossils have always been used as lucky charms, for in former times they were thought to be the natural manifestation of the Earth's creative force and not the petrified remains of ancient creatures. Fairy loaves and shepherds' crowns are fossil echinoids, related to modern starfish and sea urchins. Fairy loaves (*Micraster* species) are kept on house windowsills, with the saying that if a person has one there, then the household will never go without bread to eat. Shepherds' crowns (*Echinocorys* species) are more general lucky charms.

Adder stones are also fossilized echinoids. In former times, they were carried for success in disputes and combat. As their name tells, they were believed to be the petrified remains of frothy spheres produced at midsummer by huge assemblies of intertwined snakes. Adder stones once were held in great regard as a sure remedy against the bite of venomous snakes. Snake stones are the spiral-shaped fossils of *ammonites,* the remains of ancient cephalopod mollusks, extinct relatives of modern squids and cuttlefish. They are said to be effective in curing cramps in farm animals and humans. Built into the walls of houses, they are protective against illness.

Screw stones are screwlike fossils, the internal molds of *crinoids* (sea lilies). Many have internal holes, and thus can be strung together like beads and worn as a necklace or, alternatively, as a rosary for saying prayers. Saint Cuthbert's beads, found on the holy island of Lindisfarne, in the North Sea off the coast of northeastern England, bring good luck to those who wear them. Similar to these are star stones, which are pentagonal in form, with the feathery impression of a five-pointed star on them. They are prized as natural magical sigils.

Toad stones are the teeth of fossil fish, but they were once believed to be the fabulous magic jewels that came from the heads of toads. They are mentioned by Duke Frederick in William Shakespeare's play *As You Like It:*

> *Sweet are the uses of adversity*
> *Which, like the toad, ugly and venomous,*
> *Wears yet a precious jewel in his head.*

Toad stones were used by traditional medical practitioners of Shakespeare's day as a remedy against epilepsy and the effects of poisoning.

Tongue stones are also fossilized fish teeth from sharks, so-called because their shape resembles the human tongue. They are said to fall to Earth during eclipses of the moon, and they are charms against cramps, rheumatism, and the evil eye. The stones called thunderbolts are the fossil remains of belemnites, another relative of the squid. According to traditional lore, these are formed when lighting strikes the Earth and are used by the earth elementals as candles. Water in which thunderbolts have been laid is a traditional remedy for sore eyes. Kit-cat stones are natural black stones whose shape is the "cone of power." They are held to possess healing powers. Magnetite, or lodestone, is a naturally magnetic stone, used in former times when suspended from a string as a natural compass. Another name for it is the lovers' charm.

Colored and crystalline stones from certain holy places are valued by magicians and natural healers. Polished black stones of jet, coal, and obsidian are used as natural mirrors to reflect away all harm, as well as being useful for *scrying* (seeing into the Otherworld or the future). The green stones from the holy island of Iona, Scotland, are prized for their power to save those who go to sea from drowning. Cranfield pebbles are amber-colored stones, found on the shores of Lough Neagh in the north of Ireland, that are valued as amulets for relieving the pains of childbirth. Irish stone amulets in general are considered powerful in traditional magical healing. In Britain, stones from Ireland, especially those from County Kerry, containing quartz crystals are renowned as healing stones. But these Kerry stones lose their power if they touch the soil of another country.

Metals

Metals are found rarely in nature in their pure state. Except when they form pure nuggets and inclusions, metals must be extracted from the ore and purified. In traditional society, the smelting of ores and the purifying of metals were carried out by the smiths. The craft of the smith was essentially magical: the process of making metal and forming it into useful things was performed with magical rites and ceremonies, integrated with everyday activities. In ancient times, metals produced by these rituals were not only useful but also sacred.

Every metal has its own unique qualities, so each metal is dedicated to a corresponding planet, day of the week, and deity. Silver is linked with the moon and the moon's corresponding weekday, Monday. It brings good fortune in the areas of dreams and business. Silver rings are considered valuable in preventing cramps.

Iron is one of the hardest of metals, and it is linked with the planet Mars and Tuesday. Iron is the most magical of metals, for it has protective and luck-bringing qualities. Iron is used in traditional buildings to ward off harm, for evil sprites and demons are said to avoid things made of iron. For this reason, magical nails are hammered into doorposts, lintels, thresholds, cradles, and beds to protect the inhabitants and users against evil and bad luck. Horseshoes are made of iron, and they are nailed with iron nails on doors or above them as luck-bringers. Iron is also magnetic, and magnetized objects are held to possess special powers, for they contain the intrinsic power of the Earth, which is a planet-sized magnet. Magnetic objects are thus used to affect natural phenomena, such as the use of magnetized iron bars to prevent beer from going sour during thunderstorms.

Quicksilver (mercury) is an unusual metal, for it is a liquid at normal temperatures. It is linked with the planet Mercury, and its day is Wednesday, signifying flow, business, and communication. Significant in the mysteries of alchemy, quicksilver cannot be used either as a tool or as jewelry, but it has scientific uses in thermometers and barometers and in the rectification of electric current. Symbolically, quicksilver is associated with fear, loss, and debt.

Tin is associated with Jupiter and his corresponding day, Thursday. It is the metal said to bring one riches, honor, and the fulfillment of desires. In former times, it was used to make bright amulets worn on wedding dresses for good luck. Magically, it is seen as the metal of sudden and unexpected transformation.

Copper is the metal of the planet Venus and Friday. Like silver, it is an excellent conductor of electricity. Magically, it has the power to draw friendship and love and is worn as bracelets as a remedy against rheumatism. Love charms are best made of this metal.

Lead is the metal of Saturn and Saturday, associated with time, protection, and support. Lead is an extremely toxic substance and is thus associated with the dead. Traditionally, from Roman times onward, dead bodies were wrapped in sheets of lead for burial. Lead is also used for divination at the New Year, when the metal is melted and then dropped into water. The shapes it forms indicate what things may be influential in the forthcoming year. At sacred places, votive offerings, both requesting favors from the gods and thanking them, are traditionally made of lead.

Gold is the metal of the sun and Sunday. Because of its rarity and unchanging nature, it is a symbol of wealth and permanence, fortune and hope. Gilded weathercocks on houses, barns, and churches symbolize the spirit of the land on which the building stands, linking it with the powers of the winds and the sun.

Crystals, Gems, and Jewels

Geometrical forms exist throughout nature, at varying scales, but they are most often microscopic. Crystals are unlike almost anything else in nature for they have perfect geometrical forms that are visible to the unaided eye. There are seven geometrical classes of crystal, and each of them has a symbolic and magical meaning. Like the metals, they are related to the planets and may be used in conjunction with them. The simplest crystalline geometry is the cubic system, of which common salt is the most accessible example. It comes under the rulership of Saturn. Next in complexity is the quadratic system, sometimes called tetragonal. It is ruled by Jupiter. The orthorhombic system is ruled by Mars, and the monoclinic by the sun. Triclinic crystals come under Venus's rule, while rhombohedric ones are ruled by Mercury. The seventh and final crystalline system, the hexagonal, is ruled by the moon.

Quartz is the best known and most used of all crystals. It is available everywhere in jewelry and new age shops, often mounted in precious metals as a pendant. In Ulster and the Western Isles of Scotland, quartz pebbles are ceremonially placed on graves to protect the dead from demonic attack. The golden-yellow crystals from the north of Ireland are valued because they encapsulate the ultimate spiritual essence, the internal light. Certain quartz crystals found in Wales actually contain gold and are valuable in sun magic.

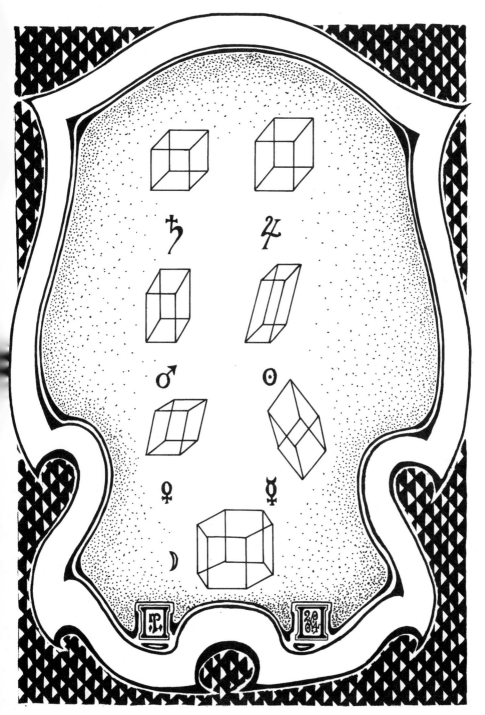

Fig. 2.1. Planetary correspondences of crystals

Sunstones, known to the medieval Scandinavian navigators as *sólarsteinar,* are of two kinds: crystals of Iceland spar and the mineral ulexite. These have the ability to conduct light. In the days before the magnetic compass was invented, sailors used their sólarsteinn to locate the exact position of the sun in cloudy or foggy weather, enabling them to navigate their ships. A sólarsteinn lights up when pointed directly toward the sun.

Fairy stones are cross-shaped crystals of staurolite, valued for their protective powers.

Gemstones are rare, and this rarity and their beauty give them value. In addition to their beauty and value, their magical properties have always been acknowledged. Like the metals, each major type of gemstone is related to a planet and, in the case of gems, to a sign of the zodiac, where it is known as a birthstone.

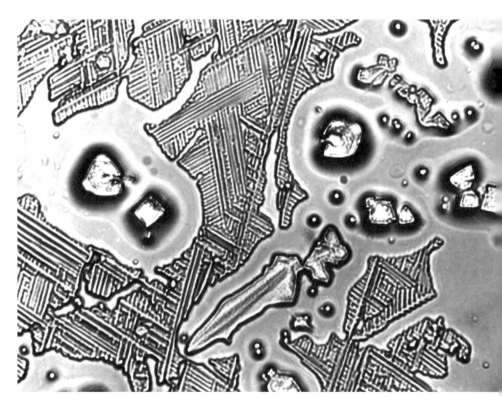

Fig. 2.2. Microscopic crystal patterns

The **diamond** is the most sought-after crystal of them all. Prized for its unsurpassed hardness and brilliance, the diamond is also the most expensive gemstone. Magically, diamonds ward off evil and promote longevity, hence their use in the crowns and regalia of monarchs (in addition to being a display of wealth).

The **emerald** is magically a gem of balance, being worn to bring harmony and tranquillity. It is the carrier of the mysteries of the alchemists.

The **amethyst** is a sacred stone, favored by priests and priestesses as a magical protector, for it contains iron. The promoter of healing during the hours of sleep, it is worn to prevent intoxication by liquor and to ward off transmissible diseases.

Sapphires are blue stones that are believed to suppress the emotions, bringing a circumspect, less selfish view of things to the wearer. Violet-pink sapphires promote selfless love.

Topaz is believed to protect the wearer against sudden death.

The power ascribed to the **opal** is support for justice and right order, warding off corruption and greed. It is worn as a magical talisman for a fair outcome to a legal case. But it only assists right and cannot win a case for someone in the wrong. The opal is traditionally the magical power source of monarchs and rulers. It connects the wearer with the otherworldly realm and is thought to be so powerful that it should not be worn on the body, but only as a ring.

The **ruby** is said to be a drop of blood from the heart of Mother Earth. Magically, in the days before the invention of firearms, rubies were worn as a prevention of blood loss in battle. They had the same function as the magical *bloodstones* attached to the scabbards of the swords of Alemannic, Anglian, and Saxon warriors. As magical jewelry, rubies are used to prevent nightmares, jealousy, and envy from troubling the wearer.

Turquoise is unusual among virtuous stones, for it reinforces the energies of the wearer. If he or she is elated, then turquoise will increase the elation. But the opposite is true. A depressed person wearing turquoise will be even further depressed.

EMPOWERMENT OF MINERALS

Metals and gems possess their own intrinsic virtues, the inner qualities that act on the world outside them. Stones can also be empowered through ceremonies. Whatever the materials we work with, it is best when we empower them magically to perform functions that are reinforced by their inner virtues. For instance, an empowerment for justice should use an opal. When this is done, the inner and outer spiritual qualities are in alignment and their power is enhanced. The connection between metals and weekdays, previously noted, gives us a means of reinforcing their virtues. Objects made of various metals should be dedicated on their corresponding days. Thus, for example, we consecrate iron tools on Tuesday, copper talismans on Friday, and gold rings on Sunday. Of course, it is possible to ceremonially empower metals, stones, and gems in other ways, but it is always best to have as many things as possible in harmony with our needs.

3

Plant Magic

THE IMPORTANCE OF PLANTS

As living beings, we humans are dependent on plants. They are the essential basis of life on Earth. All of the oxygen we breathe is generated by plants that live on land and in the oceans. Without plant life, there could be no animal life, and that includes humans. Our food, too, is the product of plant life. Plants sustain us either directly, when we eat them, or indirectly, when we eat animals that have fed on plants. Like us, plants are living beings. They undergo the same cycle of birth, growth, maturity, decline, and death, though often on a different time-scale from humans. Some plants perform their entire life cycle in a single year, while others may live for thousands of years.

The Power of Trees

Trees are the most impressive and aesthetically pleasing examples of plant life. They grow slowly, over long periods. They can grow to great sizes that dwarf human beings. Most trees live longer than the individual human lifespan, and some last longer than many human generations. Because of this, trees are witnesses to the continuity of nature, to forces that are much greater and more long-lasting than those of humans. Nature spirituality venerates and protects trees for this very reason.

Fig. 3.1. A tree in the forest

Wood, the stuff of trees, is a very useful material. Humans have used it since the earliest times for every conceivable purpose. In natural magic, we use it for many magical items, including slivers for divination, talismans, measuring sticks, wands, magical staves, divining rods, sprite flails, and ceremonial posts to set up around sacred places. It must always be taken from living trees, as dead wood has lost the virtues of life. When we cut wood ceremonially, we infuse it with our own *main* (personal inner strength) in a way that augments the innate virtue of the wood (see the section "Might and Main" in chapter 5). Because natural magic honors all living beings, any wood we need is taken in a ceremonial way. It is not good enough just to cut any branch from any tree, even if we are using a ceremonial knife and have the landowner's permission to do so. Before we cut wood, we must find an appropriate tree and then ask it for the wood. The search for a tree is in itself a meditation or a pilgrimage, which should be done in a contemplative state of mind, having a relaxed awareness of what we are seeking. When we find an appropriate tree, we wait and feel whether it is all right to cut the wood from this particular one. Sometimes it is not, and another tree must be sought. Once we have found the right tree, we first make a spell of personal protection. Then, knife at the ready, we request the tree to give us some wood, with a spell such as:

> *Hail to thee, O Oak* [or whatever] *tree!*
> *Old lady, give me some of this wood,*
> *And I will give you some of mine,*
> *When I grow into a tree.*
> *Send your virtue into this branch,*
> *That your strength will flow through it.*
> *For the good of all.*

Wood for certain purposes must be cut at special ceremonial times. Hazel divining rods, for instance, are cut at a full moon, brambles for sprite flails in the springtime, and birch twigs for besoms in September. The best time of day to cut wood is at sunrise, high noon, or sunset. Having made the woodcutting spell, then cut the branch, taking a single stroke if the wood allows it. Ceremonial cuts are made beginning below and cutting upward. Hold the branch so that it does not fall, for fallen wood that has touched the ground has lost its power. If the branch must be climbed for, then it should be handed to an assistant. When the branch has been successfully removed, thank the tree for its gift to us:

> *Old lady Oak,*
> *Accept my thanks*
> *For your virtue in this branch*
> *That its power will remain,*
> *Working for the good of all.*

Before leaving the tree, give it an offering of thanks. This can be a coin, a piece of red ribbon or fabric, a libation of ale or milk, ceremonial bread or kitchels or a candle or incense lit by the tree. If you have kindled fire, then make sure that the candle or incense is put out before leaving the tree. Once the ceremony, including the offering, is over, then the wood may be taken away. It is then ready to be empowered for our desired use. (Making kitchels is described on p. 119.)

The Qualities of Trees

Each kind of tree has its own unique physical qualities and magical virtues, recalled in age-old tradition and custom. Here are the most important symbolic and magical powers and uses of the more common species.

The **oak** (*Quercus robur*) is the most venerated of all European trees, being sacred to the ancient sky gods. In ancient Europe, oaks were venerated in sacred groves. Magically, being linked with the wielders of thunder, oak sprigs are talismans against lightning. Wood from a lightning-struck tree is particularly effective magically.

The **evergreen oak** (*Quercus ilex*), like the **holly** (*Ilex aquifolium*), does not lose its leaves in the wintertime. In the Baltic countries, perpetual fires were kept burning in the sacred precincts of evergreen oaks, which were sacred to the god of lightning and the goddess of fire. These trees were so holy that no part might be broken nor

Fig. 3.2. The Royal Oak inn sign
in Welshpool, Wales

any harm done to any living being in the precinct around them.

The **ash** (*Fraxinus excelsior*) is one of the most magically powerful trees. It is useful in divination and for making staves and traditional broom handles. The Druids carried ash staves, and it was believed that the ash warded off poisonous snakes and other animals seen as harmful. It is traditional to welcome newborn babies into the world with the

Fig. 3.3. Ash tree seeds (called keys)

protective smell of ash sap. Unusually, ash wood will burn when green, and its smoke makes a helpful incense. The leaves of the ash tree are carried as lucky charms, especially when they have an even number of divisions on each side (the "even ash").

There are three kinds of protective **thorn trees**: whitethorn (also called May trees, *Crataegus monogyna*), blackthorn (also called sloe, *Prunus spinosa*), and sea buckthorn (*Hippophae rhamnoides*). All three are powerful talismans against harm. Whitethorn twigs are protective in houses when they are placed ceremonially in the rafters. The magician's wand, or *sway,* is made from blackthorn. In use, it is held in the direction it grew, with the thicker part lowest. It is used to direct magical power. Growing wild, both whitethorn and blackthorn bushes are *fairy trees* with their own resident sprites, and when planted, they make good protective hedges. Twigs, slivers, and blossoms from holy whitethorn trees that blossom in midwinter are regarded for their healing powers. But it is unlucky to bring either whitethorn or blackthorn blossoms into a house at any time of year. Although sea buckthorn's twigs are not so easily taken, its bright orange berries can be strung together to make magically protective necklaces.

The **linden** (lime tree, *Tilia platyphyllos*) is a spiritual link between the underworld and the upper world. In mainland Europe, lindens frequently grow at the exact center of villages and towns. As the village lindens, they embody the collective spirit of the community, acting as the centerpiece of public gatherings and celebrations. A special serpentine power is present in the linden tree. In central Europe, it is personified by the dragonlike *lindwurm,* which is said to spend the middle ninety of its 270-year life inside linden trees.

The **bramble** (blackberry, *Rubus fruticosus*) is another magically valuable thorny plant. We use it to make sprite flails that are used in spiritually cleansing little-used paths and areas of ground (see chapter 8).

The various kinds of **willow** trees (*Salix* species) have strong powers of regeneration and are symbolic of purification and rebirth. The thin, flexible withies that grow from specially cut trees are used to make baskets and hurdles and for binding in general, on both the physical and magical levels.

The **elder** (lady tree, bourtree, *Sambucus nigra*) is a most magical tree, known as the abode of goddesses and gods in many traditions. Wherever they are planted, elder trees absorb and eliminate harmful energies. They are often grown by back doors for this purpose. Elder hung in sheds, stables, barns, and garages protects against lightning. But it is unlucky to bring elder branches indoors or to burn the wood. Whistles made from elder wood are used to summon spirits, and garlands of elder worn on May Eve enable the wearer to see otherworldly beings.

The **apple** (*Malus* species) bears a fruit that symbolizes eternal life, its internal fivefold symmetry reflecting the *golden section* of sacred geometry and number. At midwinter, apple trees are honored with gifts and songs, so that they will bear good fruit in the following autumn.

Rowan (mountain ash, *Sorbus aucuparia*) is protective when it grows outside the front of a house, preferably close to the front door or the path leading to it. Rowan wands are placed over house-door lintels to bring good fortune. They are put in place on a Quarter Day and replaced with new ones on the next Quarter Day. Thus, they are renewed four times a year. Crossed rowan twigs, taken from the tree without using a knife and tied with red thread, are set up on May Day to protect stables, cowsheds, and garages. Rowan crosses also protect newly planted seeds in the garden. Rowan-wood amulets are worn to protect against drowning. They can also deflect unwanted magical attacks. Rowan berries can be made into necklaces that are said to promote good health.

The **hazel** (*Corylus avellana*) is the tree of the traditional northern European bards, signifying wisdom and authority. A hazel wand is the traditional symbol of bards and heralds. Its forked twigs are used in water divining, and it is said that one will get a fair hearing in a court of law if one carries a hazel wand. Hazel poles are used to mark out sacred enclosures—*the enhazelled field*—for ceremonial or magical workings.

The **wild service tree** (*Sorbus torminalis*), though rare, is said to protect people against dangerous wild things, and its wood makes useful talismans. Another small and infrequently encountered talismanic tree, the **wayfaring tree** (*Viburnum lantana*), magically protects travelers.

The **beech** tree (*Fagus sylvatica*) is the tree of letters. In former times, it was the wood of choice for written talismans because magically, the beech stores and protects knowledge.

The **aspen** (shiver tree, *Populus tremula*) is magically protective, used to make magic shields and measuring sticks. The Anglo-Saxons planted aspen trees as markers on boundaries between farms and parishes.

Bay trees (*Laurus nobilis*) are said never to be struck by lightning. They are planted next to house doors to protect the inhabitants against illness. People sometimes protect entrances of shops and restaurants with bay trees in tubs. On festive occasions, they can be decked with ribbons.

The **maple** (*Acer campestre*) is the tree of spiritual longevity. Bowls made from maple wood are used traditionally to serve ceremonial drinks at Yuletide and in wassailing ceremonies in honor of apple trees.

Twigs of **whortleberry** (*Vaccinium myrtillus*) are used in midwinter ceremonies, for it is a light-bringer and shower of the way.

The **larch** (*Larix decidua*) is a conifer that loses its leaves in the wintertime. A tree of good luck, it is said to shelter the Earth sprites and to possess beneficial healing abilities. Larch resin is prized for its medicinal qualities, especially as an incense that promotes health. It is especially useful against muscular problems and sinus infections.

Fairy trees come into being when oak, ash, and thorn trees naturally grow so closely together that they amalgamate with one another through ingrowth. Fairy trees have a weird appearance, and the places that they grow take on a special character as places where Earth sprites may easily be encountered.

Evergreens are special trees because they are green in winter, when most broad-leaved trees have lost their leaves. Evergreens thus symbolize the continuity of life through hard times. Magically, they bridge the boundary between life and death.

Holly (*Ilex aquifolium*), a broad-leaved evergreen, is the magic tree of midwinter, indelibly associated with Yuletide celebrations, for holly is a protective plant against all bad luck and harm. After Yule, a sprig of holly kept at home will continue its protective powers. As a physical protector, holly wood is made into powerful clubs and cudgels, used in the traditional northern European martial arts.

The **ivy** (*Hedera helix*) is another broad-leaved evergreen. When it grows on the walls of a building, it provides the inhabitants with defense against psychic attack. In former times, food was served from ivy-wood bowls as a remedy against the whooping cough.

The **spruce** (*Picea abies*) is best known as the Christmas tree, symbolizing the continuity of life through the darkest period of the winter. In former times, the resin from the spruce was equated with the rare South Arabian incense, frankincense. Spruce resin was collected and then buried in an anthill for a while, where the formic acid from the ants improved its qualities. Its primary use is in treating rheumatic disorders.

The **European silver fir** (*Abies alba*) is a magically protective tree that wards off ghosts and other harmful beings. Burned as incense, the resin and leaves give energy to the human body and strengthen its nervous system. In former times, Strasbourg turpentine, a product of the silver fir, was used as a remedy against rheumatism and wounds.

The **juniper** (savin, *Juniperus communis*) provides twigs that are talismanic against the evil eye. Its smoke has a number of distinct qualities. It is a disinfectant and so was used in sickrooms in the days before chemical antiseptics were developed. It also promotes psychic abilities, aiding clairvoyance and prophetic visions. Juniper incense is made from a mixture of leaves and berries, assisted by resin from the spruce tree (*Euonymus europeaeus*). The incense smoke of juniper is also effective in combating demons, and sprigs of the plant laid ceremonially in the foundations of a building protect the future inhabitants against disharmony.

Scotch pine (deal, *Pinus sylvestris*) is a tree of indication and illumination. In former times, it was planted as a way-marker on cross-country paths, so that wayfarers would know that they were on the right track. Its resin is used as rosin on violinists' bows, and when burned, it produces a dense smoke that is used as a strong magical incense. The overlapping scales of pine cones symbolize the protective and generative powers present in the universe. When Scotch pine cones or bark are burned, the fragrance produced helps to strengthen the might of the human body. The resins from other species of pine are also useful, though not so effective.

The **yew** (*Taxus baccata*) is the longest-lived tree in Europe. It is associated with holy ground, growing in graveyards and churchyards, where some yews are said to be over two thousand years old. It is a very poisonous tree. No part of it should be used as medicine or incense. It is very dangerous to breathe the vapor of the red resin that oozes out in hot weather, though this is said to have been done in the past by those who wanted to see visions. Yew should never be burned on ceremonial fires, for its smoke is lethal.

Mistletoe (*Viscum album*) is special because it does not root in the earth, but grows semi-parasitically on other trees. As a bringer of peace and harmony, mistletoe is best known from the Yuletide custom of kissing beneath the plant. Although people kiss beneath cut boughs that have been hung up, kissing beneath a living tree on which the mistletoe is growing brings the greatest benefit. Superficially similar in appearance to mistletoe, but wiry and black, are *witches' brooms*. Caused by parasites, these cancerous-like growths on birch and other trees can be used, like the human-made besoms, for ceremonial sweeping (see chapter 8).

Herbs

Herbs are important in cooking, traditional medicine, and magic. Herbalism is a major study, and space does not allow more than a mention of a few of the more significant magical herbs. Almost every wild plant has some use, discovered over thousands of years by countless generations of wise women and men. Herbs taken medicinally, like the active parts of trees, should only be used in consultation with a recognized herbalist. Herbs work; they are not a game. Many are tried and tested effective remedies, even when modern medicine has produced more convenient and sometimes more effective alternatives. Readers who want to use herbs effectively and responsibly would do best to enroll in a reputable herbal course of study.

Certain herbs are dangerous or even lethal when used without expert consultation. Many are difficult for the layperson to identify with certainty, and many popular guidebooks have insufficient information to allow positive identification of unfamiliar plants. Herbs growing by roadsides or on derelict industrial land may also be contaminated with heavy metals, pesticides, and other toxic substances. As with herbal medicine, so with magic. Contaminated plants may no longer have the spiritual virtues that we need. So it is better to grow one's own magical herbs when possible or to buy them from a reputable vendor.

Magically, herbs function like other amulets and talismans. **Honeysuckle** (*Lonicera caprifolium*), hung around windows and doors on May Day, is a benevolent charm. **Groundsel** (simpson, grundy swallow, *Senecio vulgaris*) is traditionally worn as a charm against the evil eye and is burned as a purifying smoke in houses at midsummer. If they are hung over windows and doors on Midsummer's day, bunches of **Saint John's wort** (*Hypericum perforatum*) cleanse and protect the house. Flowering **yarrow** plants (milfoil, old man's pepper, *Achillea millefolium*), strewn across the thresholds of houses, are believed to prevent bad people from entering. It is said that a cushion filled with yarrow cannot be sat on by a person having evil intentions.

The magic **mandrake** (*Mandragora officinarum*) is a member of the botanical family that includes the tobacco, potato, and woody nightshade plants. It has a strangely shaped root that resembles the human form, and in former times, it was believed to shine at night like a lamp. Because of this and its medicinal qualities, it is an important plant in traditional natural magic. The roots have two forms, man and woman (mandrake and womandrake). Womandrake roots are used as charms by women to promote childbearing, to bring prosperity, and to give a lover the object of his or her heart's desire. Magically, mandrake roots are used in ceremonies to find out secrets or to locate lost property.

In former times, it was considered dangerous to uproot a mandrake plant because to do so was believed to bring certain death within the year. Magicians devised a technique to overcome this. They tied a dog

Fig. 3.4. The magical root of the mandrake,
Cambridgeshire, England

to the plant and caused the dog to uproot it. In doing this, it was necessary to stop up one's ears because the plant gave a hideous shriek when uprooted and hearing the shriek was dangerous.

Today, this danger seems past. People grow mandrakes and harvest them like any other plant, seemingly without ill effects. As a charm, the root of the **black bryony** (*Tamus communis*) is often substituted for the mandrake. Black bryony has the same humanoid appearance, but is poisonous.

4

Magical Animals
and Birds

THE POWER OF THE ANIMAL KINGDOM

As living beings, we humans share our experience of existence with the animal kingdom, of which we are part. Humans have used animals for thousands of years. Today, some are hunted or farmed and killed as food; others are kept for their products, such as wool or eggs, or because they are useful or pleasing to us in some way. Biologically, human beings are closer to other animals than they are to plants, and so it is on the magical level, too. Each animal lives in its own habitat in its own special way. It has its characteristic shape, lifestyle, and instinctive behavior, which are expressed in the magical powers we ascribe to it.

The different types of animals and birds each have their own distinct characteristics. Many are so well known that they are immediately recognizable to humans. Human behavior is often described in animal terms, for we humans can relate closely to certain animals or birds. Individual human beings are often compared, favorably or unfavorably, with animals, and some animal names are used as insults, such as calling a woman a "cow" or a man a "pig" or a "snake." In some cultures and religions, certain animals are considered holy or unclean. Traditional spirituality, however, is different, for it views no animal as unclean, for nature is whole and self-sufficient.

Different animals have their own magical qualities, abilities, and virtues. Magically, these are called *animal powers.* By studying, understanding, and coming into alignment with these animal powers, we can develop our own personal magical relationship with them. Traditional spiritual techniques, such as shamanism and spiritual horsemanship, rely heavily on the cultivation of appropriate animal powers. More generally, these techniques provide their individual users with direct spiritual connections with the power of a certain animal, which become the individual's *animal helper.*

Myths and folktales from the world over tell how human beings in need are assisted by animal helpers to survive difficult times or arduous journeys. Symbolically, the animal represents a part of ourselves that we need in times when our conscious mind or our individual willpower is not enough to get us through. Animal helpers are often already present within us, for it is through the inner image of the animal that we can contact these necessary powers. We may also project the animal helper image outward onto real animals that we encounter. This helps us to retain the connection. One's *fetch,* a detached part of our individual personal existence, can appear in the form of an animal helper (for more details of the fetch, see chapter 5).

CONTACTING ANIMAL HELPERS

It is not too difficult to discover your own personal animal helper. The kind of animal will depend on your personal pathway. For example, those on the path of wisdom should seek out perceptive beasts, such as owls, foxes, martins, and polecats. Practitioners of the martial arts have a rapport with ravens, other birds of prey, and predatory animals in general, especially those whose fighting styles they emulate. Hunters relate to their dogs and horses, and sometimes to the hunted animals, too, especially in traditional societies. Wise women traditionally commune

Fig. 4.1. The swan and the crow, two birds of
different character and power

with cats, pigeons, and seagulls. It is rare for humans to have a spiritual
relationship with insects and other small creatures. Bees, as domesticated animals, are the exception.

If possible, observe real animals to see how they behave under
different circumstances. When you are familiar with the nature of
your animal helper, you can contact and experience its power through
spiritual exercises. First, sit in a comfortable posture and go into a
meditative state of consciousness. Visualize an inner image of the animal. Then visualize yourself as it. Take on its size, shape, and inner
body knowledge. Experience what it actually is to be the animal. Feel
the earth beneath the animal's feet or, if it is a bird, the air rushing
through its feathers. Take yourself on an inner journey in the form of
your chosen animal. Explore how the animal reacts to different surroundings, what emotions it has, and how these relate to your own
emotions.

When you have done this a number of times, you will be familiar with the inner nature of your animal helper and be able to call on its power at will when you need it. Once one has a personal animal helper, then it is traditional to keep its awareness present by wearing or carrying some reminder of the animal. Amulets made from teeth, claws, feathers, or bones link the wearer to his or her corresponding animal power. If an actual part of an animal is inappropriate, then a symbolic representation is just as good.

When you have an animal helper, it is important to remember that you are still a human being. When we deal with animals in this way, regression to a subhuman state is an ever-present possibility. Regression is not the aim of natural spirituality, which goal is spiritual progress to a state of higher consciousness.

Bird Magic

Every spiritual tradition on Earth associates the birds of the air with spiritual powers. Deities and human shamans have been said to use birds as messengers or as means of spiritual travel. Polytheistic religions refer a specific kind of bird to each goddess and god. The attributes of the bird reflect in some way the powers of the deity. In ancient Italy, the Etruscan *augurs* determined the inner qualities of places from the location and direction of flight of flocks of birds. In medieval central Europe, Jewish magicians wrote magic squares for flying in the air in the form of a bird, or rather for magically transferring their awareness into a bird so they could view the world from above.

When birds fly, they are in total harmony with the winds and the weather. So traditionally, their behavior is observed to see how the weather is going. When **house martins** (*Delichon urbicum*) fly low, then rain is imminent, or when **seagulls** (*Larus* species) dip their heads in the sea, then a gale is blowing up. It has always been an important part of the European tradition to observe the flight of birds, the pattern of their flocks, and the part of the sky in which they are flying. From these signs, it is possible to foretell the weather, gain omens for an undertaking, or determine whether a place is beneficial or harmful to animal and human life.

Certain birds have special magical attributes. These come from the actual character of the bird itself or are explained by myths. The **crane** (*Megalornis grus*) has been a significant power-bird for many thousands of years. Images of cranes appear on Celtic and Roman altars, and its movements are the origin of the human ceremonial crane dance in labyrinths. The crane is a symbol of watchfulness. It guards entrances to the Otherworld, both the world of nonhuman spirits and the world of the dead. Similar attributes are given to **herons and storks** (order Ciconiiformes), also long-legged stalkers. Celtic magicians carried a magic bag made from the skin of a crane. In it were their magical power objects, used in divination. For this reason, traditional Celtic mysteries are sometimes called *the Crane Bag of Secrets*.

Like the crane, the **owl** (order Strigiformes) is also a symbol of watchfulness, but by night rather than by day. It is the sacred bird of wisdom—the "wise old owl." **Eagles**, especially the **golden eagle** (*Aquila chrysaetos*), are symbols of divine and earthly power as well as being keen watchers from above. They have appeared in military and imperial regalia since Roman times. The eagle's power of flight, and its seeming capability of flying to the sun, made it especially sacred to solar and sky gods. In myth, gods, shamans, and magicians fly on the back of eagles, or in eagle form, across the Earth and from this world into other ones. In this aspect, the eagle symbolizes transcendent, out-of-the-body flight.

Geese (*Anser* species) are guardian birds because they give vocal warnings when strange people or wild animals are near. **Swans** (*Cygnus* species), among the largest birds that can fly, have a close relationship with humans. Ancient magical myths tell of people who are transformed into swans or have swanskin costumes that enable them to fly.

Like the crane, the **cockerel** or **rooster** (*Gallus gallus domesticus*) is another symbol of watchfulness. He heralds the dawn with his crowing, and golden cockerel images adorn church steeples, glinting in the morning sunlight. Roosters also represent a virile, ruling power, for they fight one another for precedence over the hens. Cockiness, however, has its risks. He who takes the rooster's role must continually defend his position, until, inevitably, he loses to a superior opponent and is cast down.

The **wren** (*Troglodytes troglodytes*), "the king of all birds," is a holy bird according to ancient beliefs. It became the king of all birds when it hitched an unauthorized ride on the back of the soaring eagle, and thus surpassed it in height to become the highest flier of all. This legend tells us that however small we might appear, we can achieve great things by ingenuity.

The Power of the Toad

The **toad** (*Bufo* species) is an important animal in natural magic, for it bestows power. Toads can live both on land and in water, and they thus symbolize the power of transformation from one shape or one life-form into another. A certain bone from a toad, when prepared properly, is said to give the *toadswoman* or *toadsman* power over farm animals such as horses and pigs. It also gives a toadswoman power over men, and a toadsman power over women! It also provides the user with the ability to see in the dark and to see the color of the wind as well as to smell it. The bone is obtained by putting a dead toad in an anthill until only the skeleton remains. Then take the skeleton at midnight to a stream that runs from north to south. Throw the bones into the water and watch for a bone that floats against the current. This is *the bone*—the magic toad's bone. Such bones are worn on the body, strung together to make necklaces, or carried in a special way by practitioners of horse whispering, whose powers of controlling "untameable" horses or curing sick ones are legendary.

Serpents

Many people are frightened of snakes. This is wise because certain species of snake are the most poisonous animals known. But snakes also have their good points. In the Baltic countries, the nonpoisonous **žaltys** (grass snake, *Natrix natrix*) is a holy animal, which no one will harm. They are fed ceremonially at certain sacred festivals and in former times were looked after by the priestesses who tended the holy fires in the evergreen oak groves. Because serpents shed their skin periodically and are thus renewed, they symbolize rebirth and healing. The symbol of the medical profession is the staff and serpent of the Greek god of healing, Asklepios.

Cats and Dogs

Cats and dogs, our most immediate animal helpers, are the most common domestic animals. In the natural magical tradition, cats, dogs, and other animals that live with us are close to humans, not as pets, but as familiar animals. The image of the witch's familiar, recalled in countless images, simplifies and distorts the relationship between nature magicians and their animals. Familiars are animals with which an individual has a mystic rapport—true animal helpers on a spiritual level. Our relationship with them is more than just ownership.

Cats are particularly magical animals. They were domesticated in North Africa in prehistoric times and have lived with humans for countless generations. In ancient Egypt, cats were sacred animals with a special role in religion. There was even a cat goddess, Bast, to whom they were dedicated. When these cats died, they were mummified and laid to rest ceremonially in lavish tombs. Many wonderful statues of Egyptian sacred cats still exist. European folklore ascribes exceptional powers to cats. For instance, cats are independent, can see in the dark, possess a sixth sense, and appear to be almost immune to accidents, thus having their mythical "nine lives." In addition to these magical virtues, cats often have an uncanny rapport with their human companions.

Dogs have been around humans for as long as cats, perhaps longer. They, too, are thoroughly domesticated, though their origin as wild, wolflike creatures is obvious. Dogs are less independent than cats. They are fiercely loyal and can be trained to be obedient and serve their human masters. Dogs are kept as companions, guides, and guards as well as for helping humans in hunting and other sporting activities. Because of this, the dog's magic is guiding and protective.

Horses

Because human beings have bred them for riding, **horses**, like cats and dogs, have a special relationship with humans. In ancient times, sacred horses were kept in temple enclosures among the Slavic and Germanic tribes in mainland Europe and England. They were honored and well treated, and no man was allowed to ride them. Symbolically, the horse is the carrier of shamans and magicians to the Otherworld.

Cattle

Wild cattle, **bison**, **buffalo**, and the now-extinct **aurochs** symbolize untameable strength. As animal helpers, they assist us magically in breaking through difficult barriers. Domesticated cattle are symbolic of wealth. In the days before money was invented, wealth was often measured by how many head of cattle a person possessed. This primary importance of cattle in ancient society is recalled in ancient writing. The first and most important letters of the Hebrew, Greek, and runic alphabets, which signify disposable wealth, have the meaning of cattle. The actual characters are derived from a pictogram of a horned cow's head.

Swine

Although some religions consider pigs to be unclean beasts, the **pig** has always played an important part in the European spiritual world.

Traditionally, pigs are used to find things in the earth, digging in the ground for tasty truffles and buried treasure alike. Sacred to the Greek harvest goddess Ceres, the Celtic goddess Ceridwen, and the Norse fertility deities Freia and Frey, they were also valued by the early Christian monks who followed Saint Anthony of Egypt.

Rabbits and Hares

The **rabbit** is synonymous with fertility and cowardice, but the **hare** is far more attractive. A sacred animal of the ancient Celts, the hare is the epitome of speediness and is magically connected with the moon. The hare's former magical pet name, Pussy, has now been wholly transferred to cats. With cats, hares are the animals most likely to be wise women's familiars.

Bears, Wolves, and Other Wild Beasts

Wolves, **bears**, **wild boars**, **rams**, and **lions** play an important role in the European martial arts, which have traditional styles of fighting based on the movements of those animals. In ancient times, young men wishing to join a warrior fraternity underwent an initiation test that involved stalking the wild animal and killing it without the use of metal weapons. By killing the beast, the young warrior established his magical identification with it and his right to be a member of the animal warrior band. Later, during the age of chivalry, the animal connection existed in the epithets of medieval European kings such as Richard Coeur de Lion (Lion Heart) of England and Heinrich der Löwe (the Lion) of Saxony. In European heraldry, these animals appear on the shields of various families and cities as their guardian beasts.

When we develop a rapport with our animal helpers or draw on animal powers in the martial arts, we remain human. We are usually in control of these powers. But they are not without danger. The old Viking warriors, the *Berserkers,* often crossed the borderline between control and possession. There are many accounts of these fearsome

Fig. 4.2. The watcher and the gray beast

fighters, who took their power from the bear, losing control and running amok—from which comes our modern phrase, "going berserk." This was often dangerous, and men under bears' rage often killed friends and family, unable to distinguish friend from foe.

Legends of men who revert to wild beasts, being transformed into real wolves, go back at least to ancient Greece. These human wolves, or werewolves, are always described as more bloodthirsty and dangerous than real wolves, for they possess the main of humans in addition to the *might* of wolves. In Viking times, the warrior fraternity called the *Úlfhéðnar* used the wolf, "the watcher and gray beast," as its power animal. Like the Berserkers, they went wild in combat and fell into an uncontrollable battle frenzy. Such wildness was only of use against individual warriors. When the Berserkers and the Úlfhéðnar came up in later years against the controlled discipline of knights and men-at-arms, they were defeated. Controlled force always overcomes uncontrolled frenzy.

As in the days of the Viking warriors, when one works with the power of the bear or the wolf today, the borderline between the human and the beast is easily crossed. We can become overwhelmed easily with the sheer energy of wildness and lose our humanity in the process. Because of this ever-present danger, natural magicians avoid contact with these powerful and unpredictable forces.

Elk and Deer

Elk and **deer** are antler-bearing animals. It is the antlers that give them their magical appeal. Many species shed their antlers annually and grow new, larger sets. For thousands of years, people have set antlers on their own heads. Cave paintings and rock carvings of people wearing antlers and headdresses made of antlers are known from Ice Age times. Traditional dances, in which men wearing antlers imitate the rutting combat of stags, are performed to this day. Antler-bearing animals are formidable opponents. Symbolically, the antlers, and simplified antler-based shapes, are magical emblems of

Fig. 4.3. Stags in winter, a Victorian engraving

security that ward off both physical and psychic harm. Items made from antlers also hold this energy within themselves. They are used for things that need secure closing or holding, such as buttons or handles of walking sticks. Antlers are also useful for making protective talismans.

5

The Power Within

BEING HUMAN

Traditional spirituality is grounded in being human. It seeks to understand what it is to be human and uses this knowledge to enhance life. As part of traditional spirituality, natural magic respects the creative life force in all things. According to the natural magical worldview, being human does not give us the right to dominate and destroy nature. Rather, it teaches us to be mindful that all things are interconnected, that polar opposites are actually two sides of the same unity. Meditation on this leads us to a new understanding of our human existence, for without this worldview we cannot work natural magic.

The Magic of the Human Body

Natural magic is grounded in the reality of the here and now, being a human being in a human body. According to the spiritual viewpoint, we human beings are not just finite, material pieces of living flesh, intelligent machines, or organic computers, but also beings who exist on many levels. Traditionally, the human body is viewed as a microcosm, a little "world" that reflects the greater—the entire universe. This is a poetic way of saying that every element of existence, every possibility, and every process that can take place exists within our own human potential. Because of this, we can relate consciously to every part of existence that we encounter, both the seen and the unseen.

Several ancient European myths tell how the gods formed the first humans from trees. Myths from different lands tell of different trees. They include the ash, elm, and oak. The common feature of these myths emphasizes the oneness of humans and the other living beings of the natural world. Because our bodies are patterned according to natural laws, natural magic allows us to live every part of life according to them. Cultivating direct access to these natural laws—the way things happen— is the goal of natural magic's spiritual development. When we achieve this goal, we are integrated with the cosmos and reflect it in every way—just as in the ancient Egyptian magical maxim "As above, so below."

Thousands of years ago, the ancients recognized that the human body has a harmonious structure. Its dimensions, proportions, and the way that it moves perfectly express the harmony of nature. Sacred artifacts, including buildings, are ideally related to the human body. The Roman architectural author Marcus Vitruvius Pollo (writing ca. 28 BCE) tells us that temples must have an exact proportion calculated from the ratios of the members of the human body. When such a holy building is made, then the humans within it are part of a larger whole that itself reflects the structure of the cosmos. Thus, true integration of the human with the All takes place. This integration is not a loss of self or identity, for each of us is personally unique in space, time, and circumstance. Thus, natural spirituality teaches us that the finite, which is within us, can contact and become integrated with the infinite.

The Symbolism of the Parts of the Body

Following the maxim "As above, so below," the magical worldview relates the various parts of the body to the signs of the zodiac. The signs are said to rule the corresponding body parts. The head, sight, and expression are ruled by Aries, the Ram; the neck, throat, and voice by Taurus, the Bull; while Gemini, the Twins, correspond with the arms. Cancer, the Crab, is linked with the chest, breasts, and stomach; and Leo, the Lion, with the heart. Virgo rules the abdomen

Fig. 5.1. Zodiac sign correspondences
with the parts of the human body

and intestines. Libra, the Scales, is linked with the kidneys and the navel; and Scorpio, the genitals. Sagittarius, the Archer, corresponds with the thighs. Capricorn, the Goat, is linked with the knees; and Aquarius, the Water Carrier, with the lower legs. Finally, the Twin Fishes, Pisces, rule the feet.

But as the signs themselves denote not only the heavenly constellations but also qualities or collections of attributes, so they are also symbolic. The relationships to the parts of the body are also symbolic. The meaning of the sign denotes the subtle qualities present in the corresponding part of the human body.

Ørlög and Destiny

Our existence is part of a process. Nothing exists without coming from somewhere. Material existence, form and its energy, on the seen and unseen levels, is the result of what went before. The sum of all of the events that led to the present existence of anything is called its *ørlög,* a word meaning both "primal laws" and "primal layers." Ørlög is more than simply the laws of nature or the record of history, for it includes all of the factors that determine why anything in existence is as it is. Every human being has his or her own personal ørlög, which includes our genetic makeup, our collective and individual history, and every other relevant factor in our existence.

We cannot escape ørlög, for we cannot change the past or the circumstances that come from it. Our ørlög also accumulates as we get older. It is the sum of everything that we do, where we are, and the events around us that affect our lives. The individual's ørlög both gives us our possibilities in life and limits them. Because of this, ørlög is sometimes confused with destiny or fate, a force that is seen to favor some individuals and destroy others.

Destiny and fate, however, are seen as unchangeable, and human beings are merely helpless pawns. Ørlög, however, is only the condition of the present, influenced by and containing the effects of the past. While this limits our future, it does not determine it, for we have free

Fig. 5.2. The body and the labyrinth

will. Cultivation of our personal abilities, on the physical, intellectual, and magical levels, including the use of divination, enables us to use our ørlög effectively and not be subjected to the random happenings of fate.

Might and Main

Traditionally the powers of the body are seen as embodied in two separate but linked qualities: might and main. Might is the physical strength of the body: the energy within it that enables it to live, powering its movements and actions. Main is the inner strength that empowers the personality. Without main, might is useless, for main includes the will to live. It is main that enables a person to exert his or her will in all realms of life. It empowers the magical arts of the human being. We must have both might and main in order to live effectively. Without one or the other, we are close to death.

Inner power corresponds with outer powers through the harmonious manifestation of being in the right place at the right time to achieve what is necessary. This is shown, for instance, in the English martial arts, whose Four Grounds of effective action are defined as judgment, distance, time, and place. To be successful in combat requires a perfect combination of these factors. Equally, in natural magic, we must be mindful of the Four Grounds. The inner human power of might and main must be balanced harmoniously with the outer, cosmic power. When both are in alignment, then the human is at one with the cosmos. Maintaining this equilibrium is a constant task.

The Cosmic Breath within Us

Breath is synonymous with human existence. Each of us began life by drawing a first breath—the cry of the newborn baby. Our regular breathing measures out our life span, and when we die, we literally expire—breathe out our last breath. Birth is thus the moment of the first breathing-in, and death, the last breathing-out. Between, we are living and breathing. Spiritually, the human being is not separate from his or her surroundings. We breathe in the atmosphere that surrounds us and partake of its spiritual as well as its chemical essence. By practicing natural spirituality, we can become aware of the subtle atmospheres that surround us.

Traditional spirituality views the human breath of life as an image of a greater whole—the universal cosmic breath that is present throughout the cosmos. This is often identified with the subtle spiritual empowerment of the physical elements known as the quintessence.

The human being possesses a mind, that is, consciousness and personality. These minds can be described physically, psychologically, and mystically, but they are a mystery that defies attempts to describe them in words. According to traditional ideas, the powers of perception, reflection, thought, memory, and inspiration are aspects of the cosmic breath. It is through our portion of the cosmic breath that we experience inspiration, by means of which magic can be worked.

The Eight Parts of the Body

Natural magic is essentially a symbolic way of understanding and interacting with our existence. Through symbols, we can achieve a form of understanding that transcends the materialism of much of modernity. The teaching of the *Eight Parts of Man,* for example, is a traditional view of the human body that comes to us from the ancient Welsh bardic tradition.

Expanding on the principles of the four elements, it relates the various qualities that make up the human being to the qualities of the elements. Thus, the Earth, which is inert and heavy, corresponds with the flesh. Stone, the hard material, corresponds with the bones. Water, moist and cold, signifies the blood, while the briny and sharp Salt empowers the nerves. Air is the breath, while the clear and fair sun, which is Fire, gives the body its heat. Spirit is the soul and life, while Divinity gives the human intellect.

Correspondingly the various human temperaments are said to be ruled by the bodily parts. The forehead signifies the sense and the intellect; the nape of the neck, the memory. The pate (top of the head) stands for discretion and the faculty of reason, while lust resides in the breast. The heart is filled with love, but anger and wrath are in the bile. In the lungs are breath, and in the spleen, joyousness. The blood holds the power of the body, while the liver maintains

Fig. 5.3. Sunset over the water

its heat. The mind is ruled by the spirit, and the soul is ruled by faith.

External Existences

Traditional teachings tell us that in addition to the physical body that we can see and our inner natures, there also are other, external connections. The concept of the separate soul that survives the death of the body is present in many religious belief systems. Astral projection and out-of-body experiences may be related to the travels of the soul or to externalized consciousness. Natural spirituality also recognizes the fetch, a detached part of our personal being that we or others may see sometimes.

The fetch can appear in various forms. It can be a crescent of blue-white light, a spirit animal, or our own double. When someone appears to be in two places at once, this is an appearance of her or his fetch. Because the fetch appears separate from us, we can view it also as a personal protective spirit or guardian angel. This guardian angel, or *dís* in Old Norse, is connected with one's bodily existence for the duration of her or his life. Some magicians believe that personal knowledge of this guardian spirit is the key to enlightenment.

Our personal *luck* can also be viewed as an external spirit that accompanies us through life. Some ancient teachings tell us that the guardian spirits give us our individual luck at birth. Magical personal luck is not the same as being lucky. We can use our luck to assist others. It can be augmented by conscious acts that bring us goodwill or improved social standing.

Empowerment

Natural magic enables us to fully use our might and main in a creative way through spiritual empowerment. Spiritual empowerment is the harmonization of the body and mind with the all-encompassing power of the cosmos. It can be achieved by means of spiritual exercises that bring the functions of body and mind into alignment with each other, and then into alignment with eternal forces. There are five stages in the spiritual exercises of natural magic, as follows.

First sit in an alert, yet relaxed position, either with the legs crossed or with the legs beneath the body. Next, regulate the breath. Once the breath is under control, regular and slow, banish all unwanted thoughts. This is not easy for the beginner. First, by closing your eyes, withdraw your attention from all external objects and distractions. Suppress the inner mental images, too. Then let your bodily sensations gradually fade and become unimportant.

It is possible to banish unwanted thoughts by

concentrating on a specific thought, perhaps the visualization of a symbol. This can be something spiritual that has personal meaning. It is best to find an appropriate personal symbol to use each time one performs this practice. Use it regularly, and it will become part of your consciousness. Once you are in a meditative state, then the next step is sound in the form of chant or song. The sacramental energy present in words is recognized throughout the world. An appropriate chant, spell, or song that comes from within will raise that energy and empower the singer. Once the activity is finished, there must be a reawakening, a reentry to the everyday world. This is accomplished in the reverse order, consciously bringing each part of the body and mind back to normality, functioning once more for the demands of life. The body, as well as the mind, will feel revitalized at the end of the process, giving us a greater awareness of our surroundings and our creative possibilities.

Elemental Alignment

A good way of gaining bodily and mental familiarity with the four material elements, and the fifth nonmaterial one, is to use them in meditation. Like other magical activities, you should perform these meditations inside a protective boundary. Each time you work with an element, use the same technique. Begin with the densest element, Earth, then proceed to the lightest, Fire, in the sequence: Earth, Water, Air, Fire.

Earth

⊕ **Earth Meditation:** Put some earth in a ceramic or glass bowl, and place it in a convenient location. Sit in a meditational posture and focus your attention on the earth in the bowl.

Explore in your mind the many possibilities of earth symbol-ized by this small sample. When you have done this, allow your consciousness to enter the earth. Become at one with it. Experience its heaviness, its many variant forms and possibili-ties, and the feelings that they bring.

Water

 Water Meditation: Pour some natural spring or well water into a bowl, and place the bowl in a convenient location, as before. Focus your meditation on the water. Explore the many forms of water: wetness, rain, streams, puddles, lakes, and the sea. When you have done this, allow your consciousness to enter the water. Become at one with it. Experience its fluid-ity, its many variant flowing possibilities, and the feelings that they bring you.

Air

 Air Meditation: Light some incense. It is best to use some that you have collected yourself, such as resin from a tall conifer. Burn it on charcoal in a fireproof dish, kindling it with struck fire (such as a cigarette lighter, not matches). Place the dish in a convenient place, as before. Then focus your medita-tion on the smoke that indicates the invisible air. Explore the many forms of air: the atmosphere of places, breezes, winds, storms, hurricanes, and whirlwinds. When you have done this, allow your consciousness to enter the air. Become at one with it. Experience its freedom and motion and the feelings that they bring.

Fire

 Fire Meditation: For this, light a candle, using struck fire. It is best to use a fire-colored one, deep orange or red. Watch the brilliant flame and focus your awareness on the qualities and forms of fire and flame: heat, flickering light, red-hot metal, volcanic eruptions, and the power of the sun. Then imagine yourself as part of the fire, experiencing the feelings that this generates.

The Subtle Power

◉ **Subtle Power Meditation:** Sit as before, visualizing the natural empowerment of all existence, the flowing energy matrix on which all things are patterned. Envisage it as ever-changing, flowing geometrical colors and forms, like the rainbow patterns on the surface of a bubble.

When you have finished each meditation, direct your consciousness away from the object. Return to a full awareness of the things around you. When you begin, it is best to work several times with each element, until you feel ready to move on to the next one. Once you have worked through all five, you will find that your understanding of the subtle realms has been greatly empowered.

MAGIC JOURNEYS

Magic journeying can be either an inner journey or an outward journey toward a physical objective. The inner journey, or pathworking, involves traveling through inner landscapes, visualizing the land and the events that one encounters there. We can do this in the form of our animal helper as well as in our normal human way. When we do this well, it can give us fresh insights, feelings, and qualities of mind that cannot be put into words.

The outer journey is similar, except it involves actual physical movement. The sacred pilgrimage is the classic example of this kind of traveling. It involves traveling along a prescribed route, taking sacred paths, and visiting holy places along the way. The prospective wayfarer must first come into the proper frame of mind and spiritual condition before beginning the journey. Once in this state, he or she will experience the unseen, spiritual side of the landscape, coming into contact with otherworldly realities.

Outer journeys need not be the equivalent of religious pilgrimages, however. They can be a spiritual exploration of a new area until the seeker finds a natural spiritual place in the landscape where she or he can have a rapport with the unseen.

Spiritual Exercises in Everyday Life

The way of natural spirituality is an everyday path. We do not put it aside, only to use it when we need something. Daily spiritual practices, no matter how short they may be, are important. They remind us of what we are and what we are doing. They also serve to rid us of unnecessary and unwanted thoughts, fears, and projections that may have been laid on us by others. Negative energies tend to build up unless they are dealt with on a regular basis. Useful spiritual practices include acknowledging the day in the morning after getting up, cleansing rooms with incense before starting work, offering thanksgivings before meals, and relaxing with meditations in times of stress.

Death

Everything that has a physical life must die. At death, the body loses its might and main. All animation, awareness, and spirit leave the body. The elements that make up the body are released back to Mother Earth. The four elements depart in a specific sequence. The first elements to be lost are air and fire. At one's last breath, animation departs, and along with it, the warmth of the body, with its power of awareness and regeneration. Next, the element of water departs. The bodily liquids are lost, and the flesh is dissolved back into its material origin, the earth.

All that remains physically for any length of time is the earth, as the essence of stone, the bones. These exist long after the rest of the body is dissolved, retaining some of the essence of the individual to whom they belonged. On the spiritual plane, what remains is the reputation of the dead person and his or her *shade,* or ghost, which continues to appear in his or her old "haunts."

6

The Magic of the Land

THE ENSOULED LANDSCAPE

Human beings are rooted in the earth, though urban civilization generally behaves as though this is not true. Traditional teachings from the world over assert that the land is not spiritually dead, but is endowed with its own life, a soul of the land. This is not a superstitious or conceited idea, for each individual does have a personal relationship with the land, whether or not he or she recognizes it. This personal relationship extends to the subtle areas of spiritual life in the landscape.

But this spiritual life is often hidden from human view, especially in our urban, technological civilization. It is expressed in symbols, rather than being directly visible. This spirit of the land is not easy to contact, for it has a reality separate from human beings. It exists on another level of reality. Human beings can and do interact with it, but its everyday existence continues without regard to human concerns. How it shows its presence may vary greatly from place to place, with as great a variation as we can find among human personalities.

This Earth spirit may be experienced in as many different ways as there are different people. It is frequently viewed as a personification, as an Earth sprite, an Earth elemental, a place saint, or a named goddess or god. These apparitions of spirit have different names in different places. Essentially, they can be understood as elementals or energies of the element of Earth, comparable with the sprites of Fire, Air, and Water. Unlike these three types of entities, which are part of the flowing, moving elements, however, the Earth sprites are located in a specific place on Earth.

Earth Elementals

Earth elementals, or "earth energies," are expressed through human understanding because it is through us that they are made known. They are known locally in different places as elven folk, faeries, buccas, bogey beasts, brownies, goblins, gnomes, sprites, cluricauns, leprechauns, portunes, pixies, piskies, woodwives, land wights, oakmen, yarthkins, and the Gentry, and there is a vast and varied body of traditional lore concerning Earth sprites in every land. Some sprites are known to be helpful to human beings and some are indifferent, while others are malicious. They are all, in some way or another, spiritual guardians of the land, with whom we must come into a relationship if we are to thrive.

Sometimes, when we are seeking a good place to be, we may encounter unhelpful or even harmful sprites at a place. Although it is possible magically to overcome them, traditional spirituality teaches that we must respect them. We must recognize their primal right to be there and try to find out why they oppose us. If it is clear that our activities are not in harmony with the spirits of the place, then we must leave and go elsewhere.

Earth elementals sometimes appear spontaneously to human beings, without warning. These landscape encounters are the stuff of fairytale and legend, giving the beholder a sudden shock of an unexpected glimpse of otherness. If we react to such an appearance in a spiritual way, then we may be transformed for the better. The spirit-guardians of certain places can also be contacted by us if we choose to do so. Whether we contact them or they contact us, the places where they manifest can become empowered by human spiritual activity and be transformed into holy grounds.

Holy Grounds

Holy grounds are places where the Earth spirit manifests in some special or notable way. Across the world, such spiritual places are recognized by people and treated with care and reverence. Spirituality without a material base is barren and lifeless; holy grounds enable us to be grounded spiritually. To honor the spirit of the place, people perform rites and ceremonies. They pray, sing songs, perform holy dances, leave offerings, construct altars, or erect sacred buildings there.

Places of Natural Ensoulment

There are certain places in the natural landscape whose spirit is more likely to be noted by humans. They are special places on mountains and hills, notable rocks and stones in the landscape, groves of trees, sacred springs and holy wells, rivers, and places hallowed by our ancestors. They are all holy grounds, at which something intangible but nevertheless real is present.

When they are treated with care by humans, holy grounds may be acknowledged as natural ensouled objects such as rocks, springs, and waterfalls. Or they may appear somehow different in a less tangible way. The grass may appear greener, there may be rare and unusual flora and fauna, or there may be inexplicable patches of bare earth. Trees may take unusual forms or grow together in notable ways. Birds and animals may be unusually friendly to human beings. When we encounter these differences, we can recognize the spirit of such places and commune with it. Those who enter holy grounds in the proper state of consciousness and with reverence, but not solemnity, have a better chance of harmonizing themselves with the unseen than do tourists who go to look and take photographs.

Springs and natural fountains are places of power in the land. Hot and healing springs have always been honored, as they are even today. But not all springs are beneficial. Plutarch, the Greek philosopher and author, wrote, "Men are influenced by streams of varying power coming from the earth. Some of them drive people mad or cause disease or death. The effect of some others is good, healing, and beneficial." But even the harmful ones have a right to exist, for the world is not for humans alone. Such places, too, are ensouled with their own individual natures. The nature of the indwelling spirit of a well or natural spring is often expressed in its name. Holy wells are dedicated to spiritual beings, gods, goddesses, and saints whose local myths and legends frequently have something to tell us about the water's spiritual virtues. These beings, and the qualities they symbolize, can be recognized and honored by us.

Within the Earth

Because we live on the Earth, are nurtured by her produce, and return to her at death, symbolically, she is our mother. When we enter a natural cave, we are entering the body of Mother Earth. Caves are paradoxical places, where we can experience darkness during daylight. Inside, the conditions change little, so they appear cool in summer and warm in winter. Caves, like springs, are places where we can contact the unseen inner realms. Within us, there is the dark unconscious that lies within the conscious mind. When we decide to enter a cave, we risk unknown encounters. By entering, we begin an exploration of the hidden underworld of the unconscious. There, we breathe underworldly air, a portion of the subtle cosmic breath that empowers all existence. For, although they are dark, caves are places of vision.

The natural magic of caves brings us into another dimension of awareness. Although we are awake and conscious, our perception is altered. Strange unworldly sounds come from the depths of the Earth. We may hear them as voices, the song of otherworldly birds, or the breathing of Mother Earth. In a dark cave, we may begin to see hallucinations or inspired visions of otherness. If it is a traditional place of seership, and as we go into a meditative state, we may learn something useful from these visions. Historically, caves have been places inhabited by oracle-giving prophetesses who relayed messages from the Otherworld to the everyday world. In caves, these powers are open to us today.

Fig. 6.1. Indwelling spirit of the holy hot springs at Bath, England.
The Roman carving is from the former temple there.

Spirit Trees and the Wild Wood

Trees are often significant witnesses to spirit, for they often possess characteristics that reflect the subtle qualities of the places at which they grow. Trees distorted by the wind or other natural forces, those of exceptional size, or those growing at remarkable locations are likely to be spirit trees. So are individual examples of rare or unusual species. Such trees are often given names by local people and have rites and ceremonies performed at them at appropriate times. Certain kinds of tree are more likely to be enspirited than others. These are the trees that are most valuable in natural magic, such as rowan and elder, ash, linden, oak, and thorn (see chapter 3).

Orchards, places where fruit trees grow, are symbols of the otherworldly earthly paradise, and, according to traditional spirituality, to cut down an orchard is an act of spiritual vandalism bordering on blasphemy. Fruit trees, like the apple, a symbol of immortality, bring a peaceful and benevolent atmosphere to the land on which they grow. It is customary each winter to honor the apple trees by wassailing, when traditional songs are sung and offerings of food and drink are left for the trees and the spirit-guardians of the orchard.

The Wild Wood that appears in myth and legend was a reality in many places in former times. The ancient temperate lands were covered with dense, primal forests. Over the centuries, these natural forests have been cut down at the hands of humans, and little remains today except the names and the legends. As a potent symbol, however, the Wild Wood remains. Wildness is often viewed as a bad thing, a state of being out of control. But this is not so, for it represents the primal state of natural things, beyond the reach of human interference. The Wild Wood is a place of eternal elemental powers, which those who enter may contact.

If we return to the Wild Wood periodically, either in reality or through an inner journey, we are offered the chance of deep inner psychic renewal. In the Wild Wood, we can contact the Wild Man or Wild Woman within us, reconnecting ourselves with our inner instincts.

Within the elemental powers of the Wild Wood, the artificiality of the everyday world of human competition and banality is replaced by the possibility of communion with nature and the promise of the fulfillment of our true natural selves.

The Magic of Landscape Features

Animals make their own tracks across the Earth, and so pathways predate the appearance of human beings. These tracks follow the best possible routes across the land, climbing hills in the most comfortable way and avoiding obstacles naturally. Ancient human paths and tracks doubtless followed the tracks of animals. They, too, are comfortable to walk, having been made in times before maps and machines had priority.

Natural magic recognizes ancient tracks, with their special characteristics, as places with potential power. They are not holy in their own right, but we must respect their particular energies. Certain spiritually active points on paths and trackways, known as stopping places, command respect from passersby. They are often difficult places, either on the physical or the psychic level. It is customary to say a prayer, sing a song, or leave an offering at these stopping places. When we do this, we acknowledge the spirit of the place and renew our inner strength to continue along the path ahead of us. This is especially important when we are about to ford a river, cross a treacherous bog, or ascend a steep slope. After successfully passing the danger, we stop to give thanks at the next spiritual stopping place.

In certain country places, the old *coffin paths* may still be in existence. In former times, before funeral directors took over every aspect of funerals, dead people were carried in their coffin from their home to their place of burial. Many places had special paths that the pallbearers took to reach the graveyard. These were known by local people and used only for funerals. Such coffin paths, or *bier baulks,* are still thought by some to be dangerous places. One needs magical protection there against unwanted entities.

Pathways of spirit, sometimes following animal tracks, can also be found in country districts. These have their local names and traditions, such as the *fairy tracks* of Ireland and the *trod* of western England. At certain times, it is considered dangerous to walk along these tracks, for otherworldly beings will be traveling along them. The inhabitants of a house built on either a coffin path or a spirit-way will be plagued with problems, so it is customary not to build there.

Crossroads and Labyrinths

Crossroads are magical places. They are places where the wayfarer must make a decision about which direction he or she must take. As central points, whose ways radiate in all directions, they provide access to the world above and the world below. Crossroads are good places to make magical changes. Using a ceremony, we can give away our harmful feelings at a crossroads and make a new start. Objects bearing harmful forces may be smashed there to dissipate their energies.

Crossroads are transition points where we can decide which way to go. Gateways are also transition points, but they differ from crossroads in that we must turn back if we are not to enter them. Liminal areas on boundaries are the symbolic opposite of crossroads, for they are spiritually at the edge. They are the "borderline cases" where the normal rules of behavior and existence may not apply. Magic is often conducted in these borderline regions, which include fords and bridges and also crossing-points, which are at the boundary between two distinct areas, a space which is neither one nor the other. The no-man's-land between opposing armies in warfare is an example.

Binding magic is a means to tie up harmful or unwanted spirits or otherworldly entities present at a place. The focused concentration of tying and the convoluted form of knots work in the magical dimension, creating empowered objects (for more details, see chapter 8). In the landscape, labyrinths cut into the turf or laid out in stones have the magical effect of binding.

The labyrinth is a ritual pathway laid out on the ground in

permanent form. It leads the visitor inward, from the everyday world to the center, the place of one's own spirit. As a symbol, it is unique, for it can be made in any size. Ancient coins from Crete bear the labyrinth, ancient ones were carved on rock faces, medieval ones were cut in turf or laid out in mosaics in church floors, and today, wise women use stones inscribed with labyrinths to induce trances.

There are a number of different traditional designs of labyrinths, developed over the millennia. Their common feature is a single pathway that leads to a central point. The path has no dead-ends, as in garden puzzle mazes, so one cannot get lost. Some labyrinths have a path that winds its way to the center, then out again. These are useful when many people wish to run or dance the labyrinth together ceremonially. With a single entrance, the number of people who can enter the labyrinth is limited. With an entrance and an exit, then large numbers of people can experience the magic of the labyrinth together.

Wherever they exist, labyrinths create and anchor energy. Although they are beautiful to look at, their true power comes when human beings are walking, running, or dancing through them, for then their spirit is energized by human activity. We who walk, run, or dance the labyrinth in a mindful, spiritual way also experience transformed spiritual awareness (see fig. 6.2).

Spiritual Protection of the Land

Spiritual protection of places may be spontaneous. There are places said to be guarded at night by *the Ward,* a watchful company of benevolent sprites that assembles at dusk at a "place of power" in the district, then splits up, with individuals going to their posts for the night. They form a protective spirit circle around the settlement, preventing the entry of bad luck, harmful winds, and evil spirits into any human community that acknowledges and honors them. They watch from traditional holy places in the landscape: small artificial mounds called *ward hills,* markstones, notable trees, gateways, crosses, and maypoles along the roads and paths leading into the settlement. Where these holy places are no

Fig. 6.2. The goddess in the labyrinth

longer recognized or have been destroyed, then the place itself is *ward-less* and open to all sorts of demonic interference and psychic attack. At wardless places, we must use magical protection or we will be open to uninvited psychic problems.

Place and Time

"There is a time and a place for everything," an old English adage says, and this is a significant magical observation. Location, timing, and appropriate action at a suitable place are the necessary ingredients of successful magic. When place, time, and person are in alignment, then remarkable things can happen. If one of these factors is inappropriate or missing, then nothing will happen. The art of magic is the ability to bring together these four factors in a creative way.

Fig. 7.1. Musician of the mysteries

7
Magic in Action

SHAPE AND FORM

The shapes of natural objects in the world are not random: they are the result of natural processes and show them in visual form. Using our human abilities, we can examine nature and learn from it. We can also reproduce and re-create nature according to our own culture and consciousness. Our traditions and customs are based on forms of action that have their roots in human relationships with other humans and, ultimately, with animals and nature. Only when human activities go blatantly against nature do they bring problems to the physical and psychic worlds.

There are magical meanings and uses for shapes and colors, sounds and music, song and dance. Ancient and Renaissance mystics noted the relationship between the proportions of the human body and the ratios of notes and chords in music. When performed according to the true principles of nature, music, dance, and the movements of the human body are parts of the same divine harmony. Sacred music and dance and rites and ceremonies serve to link us in the everyday world with themes and powers that are otherwise invisible and beyond our grasp. We become one with the cosmos, totally in alignment with the powers and forces that drive and shape existence.

Masks and Ceremonial Costumes

When we wear a ceremonial costume, we are making a statement. We are saying that we have ceased to be individuals in the everyday world, but have become the role that the costume denotes. Now our individuality is subordinated to our role. A ceremonial costume cannot be mistaken for everyday clothing, for it includes features that could never be worn in any other way, such as masks.

Masks are an important element of traditional spiritual performance. Humans have used masks for thousands of years in religious rites, celebrations, and times of festivity. When a person puts on a mask, she or he obliterates her or his own individual identity and takes on the identity that the mask represents. Others who look at them can no longer see that person's own personal identity but rather that of the mask. By wearing masks, we are no longer seen as ourselves, but are transformed into something other. Disguised, we can take on the appearance of another age, another gender, or another sort of being.

In central Europe, where the mask tradition flourishes, traditional masks are made from wood. The secrets of mask making are carefully preserved by master woodcarvers, whose art can be traced back for many centuries. For the masks themselves, special trees are chosen and cut according to traditional principles. As they are used only at certain times of year, the masks are ceremonially re-empowered each time they are to be used.

Masks are usually part of a more comprehensive ritual disguise. The mask changes the appearance of the face, but the ritual disguise also alters the shape of the individual. Ancient cave drawings show people dressed in animal skins and horns. Costumes made of leaves, fir cones, wood shavings, and the strips of fabric known as tatters prevent us from telling from the body shape whether the wearer is male or female, young or old, large or small. Almost all of the characteristics that give us individuality are taken away by traditional disguise. We may even, by putting on animal disguise, cease to appear human at all.

Through guising, we retreat from individuality and become one

Fig. 7.2. Mummer's mask and disguise, the Play of the Old Tup

with an archetype or a role. We take on an identity that others before us have also done, and in a real way, we are one with them. Guising is an integral part of magical drama. By performing magical dramas, we leave behind the everyday world of commonplace appearances and normal activities. Instead, we enter an otherworldly realm in which all action is symbolically related to the invisible world of spirit. Those who witness the ceremonies are equally transported into another realm in which normal time and space are suspended, bringing a glimpse of the eternal.

The Magic of Clothes

Everyday clothes are the most immediate sign of an individual's personality and status. Nature magicians like to distinguish themselves from other people by simple methods—"differences"—that can be a sign to others "in the know," though they may appear to most people to be the result of carelessness or absentmindedness. But these "differences" are created consciously and with an understanding of their meaning.

The traditional color of the female nature magician is red, the color of our lifeblood. For women, red skirts, capes, and caps are the recognized signs, as is a scarf tied around the waist. Rings and bracelets surround the fingers and hands with magical protection. Belts, sustaining the wearer's main, are both signs and means of raising and managing magical energy.

Power objects, such as talismans and amulets, each with a personal meaning for the wearer, bring further protection and empowerment. Some people wear their power objects day and night and never take them off. This is easier with rings and small metal or gemstone pendants than with more fragile power objects, such as those composed of wood, nutshells, feathers, and the like. For men, clothes worn inside out or back-to-front, odd socks, and other departures from logic signify the magician. Symbolically, these reversals denote the power of the magician to turn things round. By doing things differently from what is normal, we can elevate our consciousness above that of the everyday, materialistic world.

Talismans and Amulets

Talismans and amulets—sometimes called collectively lucky charms—are worn as magical protectors. When we wear or carry them, we are under their benevolent influence. Amulets are usually natural objects that possess some special power: a special object, for example, such as a stone, a fossil, or a gem. Amulets exert their power whether or not they have been consecrated. They are almost exclusively protective in function. They resist unwanted entities such as harmful sprites and unfortunate states of being, including ill luck, depression, and sickness.

Talismans, on the other hand, are artifacts charged by ceremonial consecration to possess specific energies. The nature of a talisman depends entirely on the actions we take during its preparation and the intent we put into it. Each talisman is given a function that the user knows, so that, when it is in use, it evokes its powers within the user internally as well as externally. Talismans are useful material supporters of spiritual powers. Their form frequently reflects a spiritual principle, and they give an opportunity for master craftspeople to produce work of exceptional beauty and power.

When we make talismans, we try to ensure that the magical virtues of the materials correspond with the desired use. Only when inner powers and purpose are in alignment can we expect the best possible outcome. Talismans are frequently of a practical, as well as a decorative, nature. Bracelets, pendants, and rings can be worn easily and enhance the wearer's appearance as well as her or his spiritual powers. Although talismans written or printed on paper or parchment form part of some magical systems, natural magic uses only talismans based on metal, wood, bone, and stone.

Amulets that cannot be made into personal jewelry are often carried in a special container, such as a pouch or a locket. Amulets and talismans are sometimes worn together, as on charm bracelets. Examples include stones, beads, amber, silver, gold, claws of eagles and bears, wolves' teeth, toads' bones, and snake vertebrae. Teeth, claws, and bones link the wearer to the corresponding animal powers. If one has a personal power animal, then it is fitting to choose something from it, either a symbolic representation or a part of the animal.

Making and Charging Magical Talismans

Talismans acquire the power through ceremonies of consecration. But before consecrating a talisman, we must first decide what its function is. First, we need to decide why we feel that we need it and what we intend it to do for us. Should the talisman function as a weapon or as a shield (should it be magically active or passive)? Should it attract good fortune or ward off harm? If it is to protect me, should the protection come from invisibility, so that it works unnoticed, or should it be visible, appearing fearsome? What is the talisman to be called? These are important considerations to contemplate, for they affect the style and content of the proposed talisman.

When we make or charge a talisman, we must have the right magical attitude from the beginning to the end of the ceremony. Proper mental preparation is essential. Natural magic should never be performed as a game, for entertainment, or as a joke. Performing natural magic is primarily a means to inner spiritual development, and this is even more important than the results on the outer level. In any case, magical processes will not work properly unless we are mindful at every part of the entire operation, no matter how long it takes to finish.

During a magical action like this, however long or difficult the procedure may turn out to be, it is essential to remain concentrated throughout. We must first rid ourselves of any negative attitudes, emotions, or thoughts. We must remain clear-sighted, mindful of our task. Because consecration focuses our concentrated willpower into the object, every action we take must be in accord. Any departure from this means failure.

It is customary to give talismans personal names. Like everything made by hand, a talisman is unique. It is made by a specific individual, at a specific time, for a specific purpose. It is as individual as the person who made it, and it is ensouled with that person's main. Even if the individual has made many similar ones before, they were made at other times with other materials. Each talisman thus has its own personality, and it is fitting to name it when we empower it. The name should reflect the function intended for the talisman.

As well as our personal attitude, timing is important. When we want to promote growth or expansion, we make our talisman during the waxing moon. Conversely, those connected with decline and diminution are made during the waning moon. Astrologers can recommend exact moments that are best suited to the purpose.

When we have everything we need and the time is right, we can make and empower our talisman. First, collect together everything necessary, decide on the talisman's name, and create a psychic enclosure (see chapter 1). This is a temporary magical barrier that protects the worker and his or her materials from psychic interference at this critical time. Once in the correct state of mind, let nothing distract you from the procedure. Everything necessary must be done with full concentration, visualizing the appropriate energies flowing into the talisman as you proceed.

Talismans are named with a naming ceremony, which may be used for anything that needs to be named. Once the talisman is finished, it should be enclosed in darkness. You can put it in a box or a lightproof bag, or wrap it in black cloth. Then rotate the container and the talisman within it nine times, calling on the power that you intend it to have. When you have completed this, bring out the talisman into the light once more. This moment of reemergence from darkness is its symbolic birth. To name it, first pass the talisman three times over a burning candle or other flame. As you do so, call on the powers of light and life to empower the talisman with their full strength. Then sprinkle seawater or water with salt over it, while chanting:

> *As I sprinkle water over you*
> *I name you (name of talisman).*
> *By air and water, earth and fire.*

Once this is over, the final infusing of its necessary energy is done. A spell stating the function is needed, such as:

> *(Name of talisman), who bears my will,*
> *I charge you to do as commanded,*
> *For the purpose of (state what it will do and where it*
> *   will do it).*
> *May this talisman work my will*
> *In accordance with eternal laws.*

Finally, visualize three interlinked circles over and around the talisman and close down the psychic enclosure. It is a fundamental principle of natural magic always to remove any psychic construct that we have made once we no longer need it. Close the working down with an ending spell such as:

> *Now the work is finished,*
> *Where (name of talisman)*
> *Has been brought out of the dark nothingness*
> *Into this world,*
> *In the name of the elements (or another appropriate*
> *   deity or power).*
> *The talisman is now ready, fully empowered.*

Colors

Most magical systems ascribe meaning to colors, and artists and psychologists know that certain colors have certain well-defined effects on people. Colors can also enhance or alter the psychic atmosphere of a place. So in natural magic we take great care to ensure that all the colored things we use are in harmony with their spiritual meanings and powers.

White is the color of primal purity, beginnings, and renewal. Light blue, the color of the sky, is distant and receding in art. It brings a calming, soothing, and healing effect, and so the robes of goddesses of compassion are often shown as blue. Red, the color of fire, brings energy and activity, augmenting the individual's might and main. Ochre red (Rutland red) is the color of the lifeblood, consecration, and women's mysteries. Purple, the imperial color, wards off harmful energies. Green is the color of natural vitality, the fertile power of the natural world and nature people. It links this world with the Otherworld.

Blue green is the color of the sea, of primal and unfathomable depth. Lemon yellow generates power when one's energies are depleted, while deep yellow is the color of earthly desire. Golden yellow is the color of the sun's spiritually empowering light. It helps us when we need to form a link with the cosmic breath. Brown is the color of barren earth, without plant life. It is a color of potential rather than activity. Gray is associated with the nonorganic world of machines, concrete, and urban boredom. Its effect is depressing. Black is the absence of color. Associated with night and concealment, but also with depression, destruction, death, and mourning, black is the color of choice of ceremonial magicians and Christian priests, for it negates one's personality.

DIVINATION

Life is uncertain, and anything that can help us to make it more certain is definitely helpful. Divination, soothsaying, and prophecy are the human ways of trying to draw back the veil of what is to come in the future, giving us a little more certainty. The idea that prediction is possible at all may have originated in dreams that later came to pass in reality. Sometimes people are gripped by sudden unexpected insights and visions. Then they may tell of things that otherwise cannot be known. Others cultivate their powers of clairvoyance, like the shamans and oracles of ancient times. Divination provides techniques that can enable us to see through the veil by alerting us to those chance elements that always threaten to disrupt otherwise straightforward processes. These techniques are designed to give us a reading that accesses the inner spaces of our minds. Then we can interpret the results, drawing out useful information.

Visions and prophecy are different in character from divination. We have no independent check on what clairvoyants and channelers are telling us. We must use our intuition to judge their personal revelations, for we cannot know how truthful they are. They may be saying only what we want to hear. Everything depends on their personal credibility. Divination, on the other hand, is not dependent on personalities. The techniques give visible results that anyone may interpret. No special psychic abilities are necessary.

Divination gives us a reading of the present state of things. Because we ask a specific question, it gives us an answer to it. This answer symbolically reveals the unseen forces acting on the present, which, naturally, determine what is to follow. Divination gives us a wider view of present reality than we can get with conscious thought, providing new perspectives and new possibilities for action. The results of divination often alert us to internal processes that cannot be expressed in language. With divination, we can develop new strategies for life.

Traditional spirituality does not teach that everything that happens has already been decided in advance by superior beings. This fatalistic viewpoint renders life futile and human beings pawns in some cosmic game: divination is only a means of seeing what is printed on the next page of existence, for the future already exists. Traditional spirituality is not fatalistic. The past is important because it has shaped the present. The future consists of the limited range of possibilities that the present gives it.

We live in the eternal present. Because each point in space and time is unique, then its unique quality can be discovered and understood. But because these qualities are bewilderingly complex, they can only be expressed through the symbols of divination. Throughout history, people have developed many techniques of divination, ranging from simple observation of nature to complex systems like tarot cards.

Types of Divination

Before we perform a divination, as with all natural magic, we must create a psychic enclosure and put ourselves in the proper frame of mind. Because divination deals with the here and now, some techniques examine the patterns of natural phenomena. Most basically, we can read the present from the four elements. We use fire divination (*pyromancy*) by reading the patterns of flames. *Aeromancy* gives meaning to the winds, clouds, and weather. Flowing water, its color and form, gives readings in *hydromancy*. *Geomancy* takes readings from the shapes, patterns, and qualities of earth.

Because of the vagueness of the forms, elemental divinations require considerable use of one's intuitive powers. There is always the danger of drifting into fantasy or wishful thinking. Structured divination systems give less leeway for accidental or willful misinterpretation. Liquid patterns can be fixed and examined. We can pour melted wax or lead into cold water and examine the once-fluid shapes at leisure. More structured versions of geomancy also exist, where a number of fixed patterns must be identified for a reading. Casting bones or sticks also follows this idea.

More formal systems, with fixed and recognized patterns, are most popular today. Users can get immediate results and interpret them directly. These are further from nature, though they can still be used to determine what natural magical action we should take. Ancient central and northern European techniques of divination that are related to the powers of nature are most valuable. They are the Celtic "tree-alphabet" called ogham and the runes. Both of them take natural things as their starting points. Ogham has twenty characters, each of which signifies a tree or woody plant and its magical qualities.

Ogham Divination

In natural magic, ogham divination involves cutting sticks from each of the corresponding trees and woody plants (using the wood-taking ceremony; see chapter 3). Each should be about 6 inches (15 centimeters)

Fig. 7.3. The Ogham stones

in length. With your eyes closed, take a stick at random from the bunch. The twig's wood gives the answer to your question.

The basic meanings of the ogham trees are as follows. (The order is traditional.) The birch signifies new beginnings and coming changes. Rowan stands for protection. Alder is the tree of spiritual openness. Willow brings clear views and awakening abilities. Ash signifies communication and awareness of new influences. Whitethorn symbolizes the active force of life, while oak represents willpower, courage, and the human main. Holly denotes difficult challenges.

Hazel is the tree of inspiration and understanding, while the apple signifies healing, recovery, and regeneration. The vine denotes rest and enjoyment of the results of work. Ivy tells of stormy times, success despite adversity. The reed speaks of threats and unavoidable change. Blackthorn denotes conflict and struggles, while elder is the tree of breaking down. The elm tree tells of concealed new beginnings, things that exist secretly. Gorse is the tree of new opportunities opening up, heather of personal success and well-being, and aspen, sensitivity. Finally, the yew tells of the presence of the inevitable.

The Runes

Divination with the runes is more complex than with ogham. Runes are characters, so we must use a system of divination that shows them to us. There are several historic runic "alphabets," ranging between sixteen and thirty-three characters. Each runic character has a meaning, such as "the power of the ox" or "joy." There are many kinds of runes available on the market. They range from discs of wood and ceramic "stones" to cards that resemble the tarot. All of these are more or less removed from nature. When we use them, we remove the chance of more than one rune of any kind turning up.

Because the patterns of the runes (and characters of other magical alphabets) appear in the natural world, it is better to keep natural. Stick casting avoids the disadvantages of using objects with runes on them. To cast sticks, we collect nine similar sticks from a birch or a rowan

Fig. 7.4. The Northumbrian Runes

tree. These should be around 9 inches (23 centimeters) in length and be magically charged like talismans.

To use the sticks, after asking the question, we throw them together onto a cloth. Taking away any sticks that have not fallen completely on the cloth, we examine the remainder of the overlapping sticks for runic patterns. Sometimes a rune appears immediately, and the answer is obvious. On other occasions, the patterns are not so obvious, and the sticks must be examined closely.

The most important element in any divination is the question. The same oghams or runes have a different meaning if the question is different. So before starting, think hard about what you want to know. Ask a simple, unambiguous question. Then you will get a straightforward answer. Further information about the meanings of each ogham or runic character can be found in other books by the author.*

---

*Nigel Pennick, *Magical Alphabets,* York Beach, Maine: Samuel Weiser, 1992; *The Complete Illustrated Guide to Runes,* Shaftesbury: Element, 1999; *Runic Lore and Legend: Wyrdstaves of Old Northumbria,* Rochester, Vt.: Destiny Books, 2019.

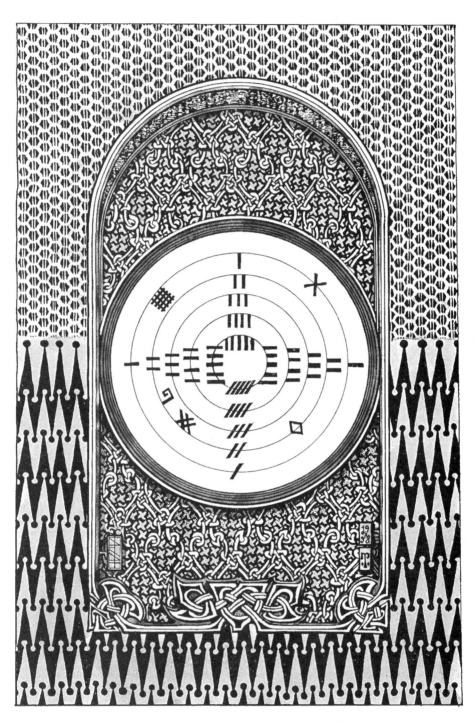

Fig. 8.1. Ogham circle (Fionn's Wheel)

8

Making Magical Tools and Ceremonies

TOOLS OF MAGIC AND PROTECTION

Natural magic requires us to have an intimate connection with the innate powers of the natural world. Magical tools are essential items for magical work. Some are more important than others. We can do without ceremonial clothing, but not without a magical knife. We use magical knives for cutting wood, gathering herbs, cutting bindings, and carving signs and symbols.

It is best not to use a ready-made knife in magical work. Neither is it advisable to use someone else's magical knife. Magical knives need to be made with as much ceremony as possible, from materials that have never been used before. Most of us are not metal smiths, so we must obtain a ready-made blade from a supplier or order one from a smith. Iron or steel blades are best. The traditional measurement is 9 thumbs in length (about 10 inches, or 25 centimeters), the blade measuring 5 thumbs and the handle 4.

The handle must be made from a natural substance: wood, horn, tusk, or bone—not plastic. Be aware of the origin of the material. Never use horn or tusk from an endangered species. The best wood to use comes from ash, blackthorn, hazel, or rowan, though any serviceable hardwood will do. Use the wood-taking ceremony (see "The Power of Trees," chapter 3) and allow the wood to season properly before making the handle.

Knife making is a magical ceremony, so go through the stages of personal spiritual empowerment and create a psychic boundary before starting. It is customary to give the knife a personal name (as with talismans, drums, and other magical items). In addition to the magical knife, some practitioners use a small sickle, called a *boleen,* for gathering magical herbs. If you have one, it should be made and empowered in the same way as a knife.

Apart from metal knives, the tools of natural magic are made from natural materials that already contain the powers we need. When we need to drive away harm from a place, for example, we use hard, thorny materials. The bramble (blackberry, *Rubus fruticosus*) provides us with just such a magical tool—the sprite flail.

To make a sprite flail, we cut nine bramble branches, well covered with thorns. They must come from the same plant, using the wood-taking ceremony. Each should measure about an ell in length (26.5 inches, or 67 centimeters). Then we bind them together at their lower end, using the bark of a willow tree. We use sprite flails to ceremonially cleanse pathways, entrances, and passages that no human has used for a long time. Holding the sprite flail in the left hand, we sweep it back and forth in front of us as we walk along, making nine passes at places we feel to be particularly difficult.

Magical Sweepers

Besoms and the tree outgrowths called witches' brooms are also used magically for cleansing surfaces. Best known as the witches' broomstick, besoms are made from three woods. The *stale,* the staff or handle of the besom, is made from a straight pole of wood from the ash tree (*Fraxinus excelsior*), which symbolizes stability. Twigs of birch (*Betula pendula,* or sometimes hazel: *Corylus avellana*) and rowan (mountain ash, *Sorbus aucuparia*) are tied to this handle by

Fig. 8.2. The broom dance: the late Cyril Papworth dancing
in Cambridge on Plough Monday, January 1997

strips of willow (see "Tying and Binding," p. 103). It is these twigs
that sweep away harmful sprites and bad luck. Birch is the tree of
purification, hazel stands for consciousness and wisdom, while rowan
protects magically against all harm. Besoms are used ceremonially
at certain times of year to sweep bad luck from houses. There are
also magical ceremonial dances using the broomstick, performed to
this day in England in Herefordshire, Cambridgeshire, and Suffolk.
The image of the witch riding on her broomstick comes from
these dances.

Magical Staves, Sticks, and Wands

Staves, sticks, and wands are used frequently in the ceremonies of traditional spirituality. The ceremony for cutting wood has been described

in chapter 3. Cutting wood ceremonially enhances the power already present in the wood, preparing it for its new use. There are a number of different ceremonial wooden tools, made from different woods or different parts of the tree.

Staves are often made from entire saplings, using the root end as the knob at the top. The sapling is dug up whole, using the wood-taking ceremony. Special staves can be made by pinning down the sapling as it grows, so that the lower part eventually forms a bent handle shape. This process can take upward of five years to complete. A stick is the size of a walking stick or smaller; a wand is a stick usually an *ell* or less in length; a stave is the height of a person or slightly less. Because the sapling has had so much personal magical attention during its growing period, its wood will be strongly empowered. Various types of wood are suitable. Croomsticks are staves with a curved top like a shepherd's crook. They are used for laying out magical enclosures, protecting against psychic attack, and hooking down holy plants such as mistletoe and witches' brooms.

We make wands from straight hazel (*Corylus avellana*) or blackthorn (also called sloe, *Prunus spinosa*) branches. Their traditional measure is an *ell* (26.4 inches) in length. A wand is used to project energy toward whatever the magician points it at. Mete wands are measuring sticks, also an ell in length and about a thumb in width, on which sacred measurements are carved. They are used to check the dimensions of certain sacred objects, such as wands.

Divining Rods

Divination is part of natural magic, giving us another dimension of perception. Water divining is one of the most direct forms of divination. We use two traditional kinds of rods to find underground water. The familiar dowsing rods are made from forked hazel twigs, cut at a full moon, preferably on a Wednesday. We hold the two ends of the fork in the hands, and the presence of subterranean water is indicated when the rod moves either downward or upward. Rhabdomantic rods are an

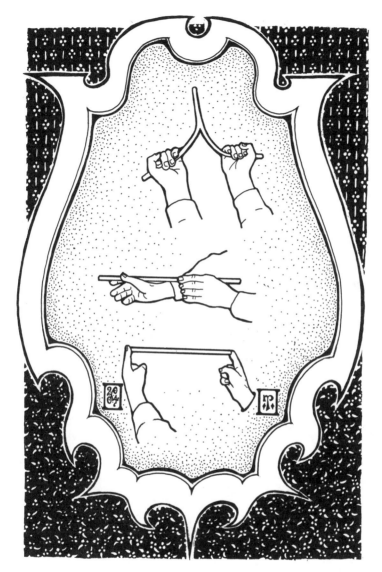

Fig. 8.3. Ways of using divining rods

ell in length. They are also taken from hazel trees at a full moon. The rhabdomantic rod is held by one hand out in front of the body. When water is present, a slight turning force will be felt. Lost property can also be found with a rhabdomantic rod made from the wood of the yew tree (*Taxus baccata*).

Fig. 8.4. Magical support

Forked sticks of hazel, blackthorn, or hawthorn (*Crataegus monogyna*) are also used to support magical objects. These are pushed into the ground at places where psychic protection is needed. They may have two branches for smaller objects, such as crystals or eggs, or three branches for larger containers, such as libation bowls or incense burners.

Tying and Binding

Just as string tied in knots binds up physical objects, so too in natural magic we can tie up things on the nonmaterial level. Whenever we tie a bow or a knot, we must use our concentration. When we are aware of it, this focused concentration also creates an effect in the spiritual realms. We can tie knots knowingly, and in natural magic, we use this power to create empowered objects.

Natural magic uses a knotted cord with nine knots, both as a protective object and as a meditative aid. To make one, obtain a length of red cord measuring one ell. To empower it, first cleanse the cord magically within a psychic enclosure. Then tie nine single knots in it, at an equal distance from each other, beginning at one end. (If necessary measure and mark the spaces beforehand.) As you tie the knots, chant the following spell:

> *By knot of one, it is begun.*
> *By knot of two, the power comes through.*
> *By knot of three, so must it be.*
> *By knot of four, the power will store.*
> *By knot of five, the power's alive.*
> *By knot of six, the power to fix.*
> *By knot of seven, the power to leaven.*
> *By not of eight, tie up the fate.*
> *By knot of nine, what's done is mine.*

The knotted cord is then enclosed in darkness (as with a talisman) and named. Once it is empowered, one can wear it as a protective belt during magical ceremonies and as an aid to meditation.

As previously noted, besoms are made by using strips of willow to bind twigs of rowan and either birch or hazel to an ash staff. The willow binding fixes the whole together, preventing the twigs from coming loose. Binding is an important element in natural magic, in which we make a symbolic object that ties up a bad thought or energy. Glory twigs are a good example. They are used as magical protection against human and demonic interference. During the waxing moon, take a twig each from an oak, an ash, and a thorn tree, using the wood-taking ceremony. They should measure no more than 3 inches (7.62 centimeters) in length. Bind them together with red thread, with the spell:

> *Thread, bind up these glory twigs*
> *To tangle up the bane.*
> *Let not a jiece* remain.*

The thread should always be from a natural material, such as cotton, linen, hemp, or silk, never a manmade fiber. Bind the twigs together with two tight bindings, one at each end, making a small fagot. Then place it mindfully at the place where protection is needed. In a house, this may be over a door or on a window ledge where harm may enter. Or one may carry the glory twigs in a pocket or pouch. Glory twigs are only effective for one cycle of the moon. When the cycle is through and the power is still required, bind new twigs together before burning the old ones.

We also make strings of objects to bind harm magically. The most common magical string is the string of beads worn round the neck. The form of the protection depends on the material of the beads. The familiar string of onions hanging in a kitchen, a functional way of storing them to dry, also has a magical dimension. They are said to

---

*A small piece

Fig. 8.5. Chain of holeystones,
Great Yarmouth, England

ward off ill-wishers, harmful sprites, and even snakes. Strings of holed stones are powerful amulets, especially when strung in nines or multiples of nine (fig. 8.5). They must be natural *holeystones,* not ones that have had holes drilled through them (see "Natural Magic Stones," chapter 2). Snail shells are also strung together to promote well-being, fertility, and prosperity.

Fig. 8.6. Traditional binding knot patterns

Binding Patterns

The empowerment of knots in binding magic comes through human activity. It is our will and skill that gives them their intention. Similarly, when we draw or carve knots and binding patterns, we empower them. Natural magic has many traditional patterns that we use to protect places, objects, and people against psychic harm. They are forms of drawn knots. Celtic art in general uses this principle.

Binding knots are miniature magical enclosures that bring harmful influences to a full stop. The most basic protective sign is the *shield knot*, used on doors to prevent the entry of bad luck and harm. The *tangled thread* pattern is chalked on doorsteps for the same purpose. The more common forms of binding knots are illustrated on the facing page in figure 8.6.

Because we go into a special state of consciousness when we tie knots, knot tying and drawing are a means of entering the non-material world of spirit. Ancient magicians are known to have made patterns to bind and call up spirits of the dead to gain information. There is one specific pattern for this, the four-cornered lattice work, which is found as far apart in space and time as ancient Egypt and medieval England.

Knot work and related magical signs are aesthetically attractive in their own right and are often seen as ornaments. Traditionally, all ornaments have a magical as well as a decorative function. They are psychically protective as well as beautiful. This is an important principle in natural magic, where the magical also brings beauty to one's life.

Sound in Ceremony

All sounds subtly influence the environment and human beings. We may be soothed, aroused, annoyed, or tormented by sounds, depending on the circumstances. The psychic environment, too, is affected. Percussion instruments have the strongest and most immediate effects. Drums, rattles, handclaps, clappers, and fireworks can be arousing or terrifying. Traditionally, they are used to drive away harmful influences and attract human participants. Before the invention of machines, there were only natural sounds and the sounds of human work, ceremony, and play. Machines brought in a new kind of sound—noise. This sort of sound is always detrimental to the psychic environment, and it is uncontrolled.

Drums are the most primal and powerful of all human musical instruments. In all cultures, they have a sacred origin. Drumming can speed up or slow down human heartbeats. Drumbeats can modify brain-wave patterns, alter human emotions, and put people into a trance. Magical drumming techniques are complex and take a long time to master, whatever the tradition.

Ceremonial drums, like all magical objects, are made ceremonially. The materials must be correct, taken and prepared ceremonially. Wood must be taken at a full moon, using the wood-taking ceremony. It must also be left for a period to season properly. The skin must be laid on the drum at midday, the highest point of the sun. The wooden part of the drum, the support, has lunar qualities of containment, while the skin is related to the projective power of the sun. Symbolic patterns are often painted on the skin after the drum is finished. These remind the musician of the kind of spiritual empowerment that his or her drum embodies. Many drummers give their personal magical drum a name. When the drum is finished, it must be consecrated to its proper use at its first playing. Then it will always project the power invoked into it.

Bells drive away harm and amplify helpful psychic forces. From the smallest bells of English morris dancers to the greatest bells of cathedrals, they summon good energies and protect the human world from unwanted intrusions. Myths and legends of the earliest bells tell how they saved people from certain destruction at the hands of demons, warded off lightning, healed the sick, and brought prosperity to the land. When a bell rings, the harmonic sounds are the physical counterpart of the "harmony of the spheres," invoking the divine wholeness that links us with the totality of the cosmos.

DESIGNING MAGICAL CEREMONIES

Ceremonies do not just happen by themselves. They are the result of human energy, knowledge, and ability, requiring careful preparation. Because they work according to well-understood principles, we must follow these principles if we are to have any hope of success. There are a number of questions that must be answered before we act:

1. **Intention:** Am I spiritually prepared for this magical ceremony? What do I hope to achieve by it?
2. **Timing:** Is this the right time for me to perform this action? What is the proper time?
3. **Necessities:** Do I have everything I need (place, tools, paraphernalia, etc.)? If not, how can I obtain them?
4. **Content:** Does the content of the ceremony reflect my true intention? Is every element and action that I have chosen appropriate for this intention? How can I create a perfect match between my intention and my actual performance?
5. **Versatility:** If this content is not appropriate, what can I do to make it so?
6. **Energy:** Can I generate sufficient energy at the present time to perform this ceremony? Have I the might *and* the main? Or is the ceremony too long for me to maintain sufficient energy from start to finish?

When we have answered these questions satisfactorily, then we can design a ceremony that best fits our needs. When the time comes to perform the ceremony, we must be mentally prepared and have everything we need with us. In any magic ceremony, we access our hidden inner powers and bring them into contact with the outer world. It is because of this openness to the outer world, both seen and unseen, that we must create our psychic boundary (see chapter 1 for the method). Without it, we are vulnerable. We must perform our spiritual exercises (as in chapter 5), bringing ourselves into the proper state of mind to perform the ceremonial operation.

With our inner state in order, we must do the same with the outer conditions. When the time is right, we must have everything ready: our clothing, talismans and amulets, magical tools, musical instruments, texts, food and drink. As appropriate, they must be already cleansed and consecrated so that their spiritual essences are also in alignment with our intention.

Most ceremonies have a logical structure. First, there is an opening statement of intent that links us with the power we are contacting. Then we perform actions that establish this link, bringing us into alignment with the power. Following this, we take some of the essence of the power and use it for our stated purpose. Once the power is used, we acknowledge its source with an offering. Finally, we close down the ceremony, come back into an everyday state of consciousness, and remove the psychic boundary.

9

Magical Food and Drink

CEREMONIAL NEEDS

Because every time of day and year has its corresponding spiritual qualities, we can express them symbolically. In every ceremony we create, we try to bring every part into symbolic connection with the time and its meaning. This includes the ceremonial food and drink that we make and consume. All aspects of traditional food and drink for seasonal magic are related to one another. The ingredients are appropriate to the time and place. They are prepared in ceremonies that anticipate their use, empowering the food with the necessary psychic energies.

In their shape and form, the food and drink reflect the meaning and symbolism of the activity or festival. In many parts of Europe, for instance, there are traditional designs of bread that are baked at times of festival and celebration. Their designs are ancient and symbolic and differ according to the time of year they are made. Designs vary locally, but each one is specific to its corresponding time and is immediately recognized by local people for what it is.

Traditional spirituality sees all meals as sacred. Without Mother Earth's bounteousness, we would go without and die. We acknowledge this reality at each mealtime with a "thank you." What form this takes is not important, but the intention is. Ceremonial meals are festive occasions when we take care to prepare the table so that it is decorated both beautifully and symbolically. Ideally, every item on the table should reflect the nature and intention of the celebration. When this is done successfully, then those who celebrate together there will be magically empowered with the energies of the occasion.

The Egg

The egg is a symbol of potential new life, and as such, eggs are important in natural magic. Symbolically, the yellow of the yolk signifies the active power of the sun and the white yolk, the nurturing embrace of Mother Earth. Traditionally, eggs are connected with springtime rites and ceremonies because it is in springtime, with the increasingly long days, that birds start to lay. The festival of Easter, whose name recalls the goddess of springtime, Eostre (pronounced *Ay-os-tray*), celebrates this. At Easter, it is customary to dedicate the first eggs of the year by dyeing and painting them and finally eating them. Painted eggs celebrate the transition from the dark half of the year to the light. Darkness, cold, and depression are left behind, and bright, new days are here.

Bread

The importance to us of bread, both symbolically and literally, cannot be overemphasized. Bread is the "staff of life," and the words "our daily bread" have become the metaphor for all food. Bread comes into being through the spiritual process known as *the Mystery of Bread*. This is a cycle of death and rebirth. The grain is buried in the ground, seemingly dead. Then it springs to life again with new green shoots. The plants grow until late summer, when they fruit, producing new grains. At the harvest, the grain is taken from the dying plants. It is then ground up and baked into bread. When we eat the bread, we absorb the life force of the grain, which keeps us alive.

Because of bread's fundamental importance to us, it plays an important role in religious and magical ceremonies. Sacred meals always have bread as a key element. This bread is not our ordinary, everyday bread, but rather festival bread that is specially baked for the occasion in traditional shapes and designs that express the meaning of the festivity. When we eat festival bread, we partake of the essence of the festivity by acknowledging the origin of our life force in a ceremonial way.

Drink

Although alcohol is forbidden to members of certain religions and too much alcohol is harmful to the health, alcoholic drinks are traditionally part of European rituals. In ancient Greece and Rome, the rites of the wine gods Dionysus and Bacchus were accompanied by bouts of ceremonial wine drinking. The ancient Germanic and Norse sacred feasts saw the sacred mead horn circulating among the participants. At holy places, gods and goddesses were offered wine, mead, and beer. In medieval England, although forbidden, ceremonial *Scot ales* were celebrated in secret locations on ancient holy days, and in the churches, the sacramental wine of the Christian Eucharist was drunk at the holiest moment of the service. Today, the custom continues among commercial breweries of making special brews to commemorate special events, such as festivals and anniversaries.

Mead

Mead, made from honey, is a favored ceremonial drink in natural magic. The commercially manufactured drink called mead is sometimes white wine flavored with honey, so ceremonial mead is best made at home. It is a long process because natural processes take their own proper time and cannot be sped up. Honey is the main ingredient, though many commercially produced honeys will not do. They are thoroughly processed to remove any trace of pollen and wax, rendering them useless for mead making. For mead, we need unprocessed honey on the comb.

The best quality food and drink are always made from the best materials, and so the best mead comes from the best honey, which bees make from red clover (*Trifolium pratense*). The recipe requires the following ingredients (approximate quantities):

Mead Recipe

1 gal (3.8 L) water

3 lbs (1.36 kg) clover honey

3 tsp yeast nutrients

¼ tsp tannin

¼ oz (7 g) tartaric acid

½ oz (14 g) malic acid

Wine yeast starter

Dissolve the honey in ½ gallon (1.9 L) of warm water, and add the tannin, nutrients, and acids. Make up the quantity with cold water to 1 gallon (3.8 L), and pour into a sterilized winemaking demijohn. Add 2 crushed Campden tablets (obtainable from a home winemaking supplier). Cork the demijohn, and let it stand for twenty-four hours. Then add wine yeast starter.

Wine yeast starter is made by boiling ½ cup of pure orange juice with ½ cup of water, adding 2 teaspoons of sugar. Pour the mixture into a bottle and add a little yeast. Leave in a warm place. After about three hours, when the yeast has started to ferment, add it to the mead mixture.

Put the demijohn in a warm place where it will not be disturbed. Inspect it occasionally. When fermentation has finished, on average between three and four weeks, siphon off the fresh mead into a clean, sterilized demijohn, add another crushed Campden tablet, and cork it. Store it for three months, then siphon it once more into another clean demijohn, leaving behind the deposit that has formed. Repeat this procedure every three months until there is no more deposit and the mead is crystal clear. Then bottle the mead and leave it to mature for one to three years.

This long and complex process requires precision and concentration. When it is created by someone in a magical frame of mind, this ceremonial drink making produces a wonderfully empowered brew that enhances any collective spiritual ceremony.

Nettle Beer

Nettle beer is an ancient drink, often used as a remedy against the pains of rheumatism and gout. It also makes a good ceremonial drink.

Nettle Beer Recipe

2 gallons (7.6 L) nettles

2 oz (57 g) hops

1 oz (28 g) yeast

½ oz (14 g) root ginger

4 oz (113 g) sarsaparilla

1½ lbs (680 g) castor sugar

4 lbs (1.81 kg) malt

1 tsp cream of tartar

2 gallons (7.6 L) water

Collect 2 gallons of young stinging nettles (*Urtica urens*). Wash them and put them in a saucepan along with the water, ginger, malt, sarsaparilla, and hops. Bring to the boil and boil for fifteen minutes. Put the sugar in a large pan, and strain the nettle mixture onto it. Stir until the sugar has dissolved. Add water to the yeast and beat it into a paste, then add it to the mixture. Leave it for six to seven hours, until it begins to ferment, then remove the surface layer, add one tablespoonful of cream of tartar, bottle it, and cork the bottle. Nettle beer does not need to be kept for a long time before drinking. It is drinkable the day after it has been bottled.

Elderberry Wine

Elderberry wine contains the magic virtues of the elder tree (lady tree, bourtree, *Sambucus nigra*). The recipe is on the following page 116.

Elderberry Wine Recipe

3½ lbs (1.59 kg) ripe elderberries

1 gallon (3.8 L) water

3 lbs (1.36 kg) sugar

1 lbs (454 g) raisins

½ oz (14 g) ground ginger

½ oz (14 g) whole ginger, bruised

6 cloves

½ cinnamon stick

1 lemon

Separate the elderberries from the stalks, and pour boiling water over them. Let them stand for twenty-four hours, then bruise them well with a wooden spoon and strain off the solid matter. Measure the liquid, put into an earthenware jar, and add the sugar and sliced lemon. Boil the ginger, cloves, cinnamon, and raisins in a little of the liquid. Strain this, and add it to the rest of the mixture. Then cover the wine for a few days. Allow it to stand, then strain it again. Leave open for a few weeks, until fermentation ceases. Stopper tightly and store for six months, then bottle it.

Red Clover Wine

The three leaves of the red clover (*Trifolium pratense*) are symbolic of the threefold nature of existence: beginning, middle, and end, or past, present, and future. Red clover wine is a traditional drink from Cumbria in northwestern England.

Red Clover Wine Recipe

2 quarts (½ gallon, 1.9 L) red
    clove blossoms

3 lemons

2 oranges

4 lbs (1.81 kg) white sugar

1 oz (28 g) yeast

½ slice toasted bread

1 gallon (3.8 L) water

Pour the boiling water over the blossoms. Allow it to stand until lukewarm. Slice the oranges and lemons, add the sugar and the yeast, spread this on the toast. Put everything together in a bowl, and allow it to stand for five days, stirring twice a day. Strain, then allow it to stand for another three days. Strain again, leave it for three days, then bottle it, with loose stoppers. Tighten the stoppers after ten days. The red clover wine will be ready to drink in a month.

Food as Offerings

During ceremonies, such as the wood-taking one described in chapter 3, ceremonial food may be given as an offering of thanks to Mother Earth and the local spirits. Food created ceremonially is better than purchased or secular food because it has been made according to the same principles that are being expressed by the ceremony in progress. Thus, the principle of integration is reinforced.

Recipes for Ceremonial Food

These are traditional recipes for food to be used at ceremonies. Although these specific recipes originate in East Anglia, in the east of England, they are of general use, and there are similar ones from many other places. The modern measurements given here in the Imperial and metric systems are not exact equivalents, but they allow the cook to produce a reasonable quantity of these ceremonial foods, enough for a group of people. When we prepare food, we do it in the same state of mind and concentration that we need when conducting ceremonies. In this way, the food is empowered with the appropriate spirit, bringing spiritual as well as nutritional power to those who eat it.

Ceremonial Rusks

(for general use at any time)

8 oz (227 g) self-rising flour

3 oz (85 g) butter

Milk

Salt

Sift the flour into a mixing bowl, and add a pinch of salt. Cut the butter into small pieces, and rub them into the flour. Then stir in enough milk to form a flexible dough. Roll out the mixture thickly, and cut into sixteen rounds 1½ inches (4 cm) in diameter. Place them on a greased baking sheet, and put them in a hot oven (425°F; 220°C) for ten minutes. Remove the rounds, split them in half, and bake again in a cooler oven (320°F; 160°C) for another ten minutes.

Soulcakes

(eaten in November and during ceremonies commemorating the dead)

30 oz (850 g) flour

4 oz (113 g) butter

5 oz (142 g) sugar or sweetener

1 tsp dried yeast

Mixed spices to taste

Milk, sufficient to make the mixture a paste

Mix the ingredients (except the sugar and spices) together, then leave the mixture in a warm place for an hour to allow it to rise. Then add the sugar and spices, make the mixture into flat cakes, and bake them in an oven at 375°F (190°C) for fifteen to twenty minutes. Soulcakes are eaten in memory of our departed ancestors and of our friends and relatives who have died during the previous year.

Kitchels

*(sacred specialty for the Midwinter ceremonies
of the Twelve Days of Yule)*

16 oz (454 g) puff pastry

2 oz (57 g) butter

8 oz (227 g) currants

2 oz (57 g) ground almonds

3 oz (85 g) candied peel

½ tsp cinnamon

½ tsp ground nutmeg

Make the puff pastry into two equal portions, add butter, and roll out thinly into squares. Mix together the currants, ground almonds, candied peel, cinnamon, and nutmeg. Spread the filling inside one of the squares, and use water to moisten the edges of the other square. Bring the two squares together, sealing in the contents. Next, mark out the top with two lines in each direction, making nine smaller squares. This empowers the kitchel magically. Bake the kitchel in a hot oven for half an hour. When it is ready, take it from the oven, sprinkle it with sugar or sweetener, and cut it along the marked-out lines into squares. *Yule kitchels* are the same for each of the Twelve Days, excepting New Year's Eve, when they should be triangular.

10
Precautions and Remedies

MAGICAL AWARENESS

As we have seen, natural powers are present in all things. Some of these natural powers are useful in human terms and can be used as remedies against harm or for healing ills. Others cannot. Natural magic provides a means for us to identify the useful powers. Then we can use the subtle virtues of many of the members of the plant, animal, and mineral kingdoms. Natural charms and amulets can be found everywhere. It is only a matter of recognizing and empowering them.

When we understand the world in a magical way, then everything we do can be empowered magically. Because the world is often a dangerous place, there are many magical precautions we can take to avoid or reduce problems and dangers. But we must always be conscious to use appropriate measures, for a remedy that works in one instance will not necessarily work in another. Throughout traditional spirituality, appropriateness is the most fundamental principle. One size does *not* fit all! As a traditional adage from the English martial arts tells us:

> *Keep within the compass,*
> *Then you will be sure*
> *To avoid the problems*
> *That others must endure.*

In the context of the martial arts, this means that we should never expose parts of our body to an opponent beyond the *compass,* that is, the range, of our own defenses. On a more general level, this means that we should always bear in mind whether our defenses and remedies are likely to be effective in the area we wish to cover. If they are not, then we are stepping outside our compass and are likely to fail in our objectives.

BUILDING PRECAUTIONS AND REMEDIES

Buildings are not natural; they are the result of the application of the human consciousness and willpower. To construct a building successfully, we must balance human ideas and needs with the necessities of the real, physical world. Any building that comes into existence must be a compromise between these factors. If people are to live harmoniously within it, the entire design of the building, its location, its orientation, and its beautification must be related to their spiritual needs.

We can use traditional techniques to find spiritually appropriate locations for buildings. These techniques also show us how to harmonize the building with its surrounding environment on both the physical and psychic levels. The materials we use all have their own magical attributes, and these can be used to keep the building in harmony with the environment. Because no place is totally perfect, we must attempt to remedy any shortcomings and overcome any harmful qualities that are present.

Ideally every stage of building should have its magical component. When we begin building, this is the moment of inception, the symbolic conception of the house. It is best if we do this first act of foundation at the right moment, when the planets are in fortunate positions. The house then has a beneficial horoscope and functions in harmony with natural cycles. Founding a building requires a foundation ceremony that empowers the conception of the house. Offerings are placed beneath the symbolic foundation stone to magically protect and nurture the building and its future inhabitants. It is customary to deposit newly minted coins, talismans, and branches of juniper (savin, *Juniperus communis*) or other magical plants during the foundation ceremony.

As house building progresses, we use appropriate magical materials, and each new part is begun with a corresponding ceremony. Bricks can have special sigils embossed on them and be laid in symbolic patterns. Magical offerings are placed above door lintels and window frames, around the hearth, on roof rafters, and elsewhere. They include twigs of whitethorn (*Crataegus monogyna*) placed on rafters, mistletoe (*Viscum album*) and acorns as charms against lightning, and crosses or three-branched twigs of rowan (mountain ash, *Sorbus aucuparia*) hung over the bedhead.

Nails are symbols of binding harmful forces, literally "nailing problems." Hammered ceremonially into woodwork, especially doorframes, they are a means of warding off bad luck and harm from households.

Fig. 10.1. Protective beasts on an old house at Hitchin, England

Fig. 10.2. "By hammer and hand all arts do stand." Stained glass by Nigel Pennick

Like horseshoes, they express the magical power of iron. Horseshoes are nailed over doors to invoke the protective power of the moon. They should be nailed up during the waxing moon, and preferably on a Monday.

When the last tile is laid on the roof or the last thatch finished, a final ceremony of *Topping Out* is customary. This can take the form of a ceremonial meal for the builders. A green branch is hauled up to the roof and is tied there as a sign that all is finished. As this is done, the builders have a drink, not forgetting to pour a glass onto the earth as a libation to the new building. Once the internal fittings are finished, then the new inhabitants should move in ceremonially, at an appropriate time, if possible.

Windows and glass doorways can give entry to unwanted psychic forces unless they are protected. We put mirrors or reflective glass balls there to guard against it. When they have been magically empowered, glass objects containing spirals of color serve to confuse spirits and dissipate harmful energies. Most common are ornamental paperweights and walking sticks, much sought after as collectables. Glass walking sticks are actually charm wands, for they cannot be used for walking.

The master glassmakers who made them created magically empowered charms against airborne illnesses. Charm wands are hung up in a room. Each morning, the charm wand must be empowered by wiping it vigorously with a dry cloth while chanting a spell of empowerment. This charges up the wand, causing it to attract harmful particles to its surface, preventing us from breathing them in and suffering illness as a result.

Outside the house, its magical protection can be augmented by planting protective plants. Hedges of whitethorn (*Crataegus monogyna*) or blackthorn (also called sloe, *Prunus spinosa*) can provide an impenetrable barrier, both to physical and psychic intruders. The main entrance, garden path, and gate may be protected by planting holly (*Ilex aquifolium*), rowan (mountain ash, *Sorbus aucuparia*), or elder (lady tree, bourtree, *Sambucus nigra*) beside them. On the roof, the houseleek (*Sempervivum tectorum*) helps magically to ward off fire and lightning. Because it is an aphrodisiac, the houseleek on the roof also promotes joyous sexuality for the inhabitants within.

HEALTH AND EMPOWERMENT

Natural spirituality has never claimed that escape from pain and sorrow is the object of life. But it does give us a means to deal with these natural components of our existence. For at least the earlier parts of our lives, while we are strong and young, we have the potential to be healthy. Illness in this part of life is the result of imbalances, and so it is possible to rectify them and bring back health. Herbal and mineral remedies, understood from the magical perspective, can help to restore the balance we need.

Plant Remedies

All traditional remedies have their origin in ancient natural magic. When used magically, the parts of trees and plants should be taken ceremonially (for trees, see chapter 3). When we do this, we empower the plants with our own main for our intended uses. The following are the most commonly encountered plants used in natural magic.

Garlic (*Allium sativum*) is a tried-and-tested remedy against all kinds of malevolent spirits, harmful magic, and demonic interference. For psychic protection (if not an attractive fragrance!), we can use a "perfume" made from garlic and the resinous parts of the cypress tree (*Cupressus* species). Other resins also make effective incenses and smokes. Cedar (*Cedrus* species), Scotch pine (deal, *Pinus sylvestris*), larch (*Larix decidua*), spruce (*Picea abies*), juniper (savin, *Juniperus communis*), hyssop (*Hyssopus officinalis*), groundsel (simpson, grundy swallow, *Senecio vulgaris*), and lavender (*Lavandula augustifolia*) are among the most magically effective, even when some of them do not smell pleasant by contemporary standards. For details of these, see chapter 3.

Hops (*Humulus lupulus*) are used as an ingredient in beer making, and dried hops are put into pillows to promote sleep. Burned as incense, the yellow pollen of hops gives off a fragrance that also assists in sound sleep. Vervain (*Verbena officinalis*), when burned as incense, strengthens the willpower. Vervain also is said to promote dreaming and enable the dreamer to remember his or her dreams. Mugwort ("the Mother of Herbs," *Artemisia vulgaris*) is one of the herbs particularly associated with women. It appears in the traditional bridal bouquet and the magically protective *Midsummer belt,* which is woven from mugwort roots. When burned as incense, mugwort promotes decision-making through conscious thought, the unconscious mind, and divination. Inulin (*Inula helenium*), important in traditional medicine against diseases of the lungs, is burned as an incense that raises the spirits from melancholy and depression.

A traditional incense, once used to empower Midsummer fires, was mistletoe (*Viscum album*). It is not used anymore because its smoke is thought to be dangerous. Although resins from conifers other than cedar, cypress, and pine may be burned as incense, some give off fumes that are hazardous to our health. Most dangerous is that of the yew tree (*Taxus baccata*), which must never under any circumstances be used, for it is highly toxic. In any case, it is unwise to inhale any incense directly.

The *herbal bunch,* composed of nine, fifteen, or seventy-seven differ-ent herbs, is made to burn as incense. The herbs are bound together in a bunch or bouquet, adorned with ribbons, and ceremonially consecrated. Then the bunch is kept in an honored place in the house. From time to time, when incense is needed, some of the bunch is plucked, mixed with frankincense, and burned. The herbal bunch is used to spiritually cleanse rooms and is considered effective against all forms of sickness.

Healing and Harmful Herbs

For unspecific areas of general healing, rosemary (*Rosmarinus officinalis*), thyme (*Thymus vulgaris*), and peppermint (*Mentha piperita*) are effective. Comfrey (*Symphytum officinalis*), once used to help mend broken bones, is useful for bringing speedy healing of cuts and grazes. Although it is not from any specific plant, *propolis,* a waxlike resin made by bees from pollen, is used to support the human immune system and ward off communicable diseases.

A knowledge of the so-called *weird plants* is an important part of natural magic. These are the plants that are dangerous to handle with-out adequate knowledge, for they contain lethally poisonous substances. Among them are some whose very names strike fear: deadly night-shade (*Atropa belladonna,* belladonna), enchanter's nightshade (*Circaea lutetiana*), monkshood (*Aconitum anglicum,* old wife's hood), thorn apple (*Datura stramonium*), and foxglove (*Digitalis purpurea*). These are the plants of the wise woman and the cunning man and are not to be played with, for the consequences are often fatal. Under no circum-stances should these plants be used in herbalism or natural magic.

Spiritual and Physical Health
through Crystals and Gems

Many of the powers of crystals and gems have been described in chapter 2. However, I have not yet dealt with the techniques of crystal and gemstone healing. Many crystal healers work on the principle that crystals restore imbalances of bodily energies that reveal themselves as disorders and diseases. They do not claim to be able to repair physical damage, such as broken bones, and anyone suffering from a life-threatening illness should not rely on magic alone for treatment. Magic is about being effective in the real world, not an attempt to bypass it.

According to modern practitioners, gemstones and crystals have natural correspondences with specific parts of the human body. They are all viewed as operating primarily on the nonmaterial level, manipulating flows of subtle energy in and around the body. In this way, they are wholly magical in operation, unlike herbs, which have an active biochemical effect on the physical body. The gems and crystals described here are the most common ones.

Amethyst is an iron-containing magical gemstone. In medieval Europe, it was the *Stone of Absolute Power,* set in the magic ring of the Holy Roman Emperor. Magically, it maintains proper orderliness in our affairs. We wear amethyst to assist our healing processes while we sleep. It is also said to prevent alcoholic intoxication, heal skin ailments, and protect against transmissible diseases. The sky-blue aquamarine, sometimes called *All-Life,* is used to stabilize energies that are out of balance, especially in the eyes, throat, and intestinal regions. As its name suggests, bloodstone is linked with the blood and is believed to cleanse the body of negative energies. It is used to combat light-headedness and body cramps.

Carnelian, or flesh-colored chalcedony, operates almost wholly on the spiritual level. It is used to cleanse the mind of unwanted thoughts. As an amulet, carnelian protects the wearer against natural disasters and accidents. White chalcedony, or motherstone, is worn by nursing mothers to improve milk production. The apple-green-colored chrysoprase, another form of chalcedony, wards off evil and also affects the energies of human speech.

Citrine (yellow quartz or gold topaz) has various effects, depending on its coloration. Its orangey-brown variety can be used to encourage positive thought, while the orange-colored crystal assists the spleen.

Coral, classified among gems but actually the product of a marine organism, is used traditionally to heal the skin and disorders of the joints.

The emerald, associated with the alchemists, is used against eye problems. It has also been used to relieve the pains of childbirth and is worn by wives to magically ensure the fidelity of their husbands. Garnet comes in many colors, and all of them are thought to augment the wearer's will to be healed. Green garnet is best for the heart, while orange garnet improves the strength of the base of the spine.

The golden, sunlike crystal heliodor is valued by crystal healers for its particularly powerful influence on the solar plexus. Magically, it assists communication between the unconscious and the conscious mind. Heliotrope, a green chalcedony with reddish iron inclusions, is used as an amulet against wounds and the stings of bees, wasps, and scorpions. Hematite, a shiny reddish-gray mineral otherwise known as lodestone or magnetite, is a natural magnet. An ancient remedy for melancholy, hematite is often used in combination with crystals such as carnelian, dioptase, lapis lazuli, and malachite to augment the patient's resistance to various diseases.

Jasper was used by the ancients as a magical rainmaker and as a remedy against snakebite. Nowadays, crystal healers use it to improve the patient's ability to smell. The blackest of all stones, jet, has the power to ward off psychic attack, especially wishing ill of other people. In former times, it was burned as a magical incense in ceremonies for healing the sick. Labradorite is a greenish-gray mineral used in magic that tries to straighten curvature of the body.

The deep-blue lapis lazuli was favored by the ancient Egyptians, who called it *the Stone of the Heavens*. It is said to be a fine remedy for many ills. As a jewel, it is given to shy children to bolster their confidence. Crystal magic uses lapis lazuli to transfer health-giving powers from the healer's body into the patient. In former times, moonstone (also called water opal or wolf's eye) was used as a remedy against mental illness. Magically, moonstone relates to the emotions. It inspires the power of love, reveals enemies, and cements personal relationships. Hung on fruit trees at blossom time, moonstone magically ensures a bumper harvest.

The glasslike stone obsidian is used as a magic mirror. Seers use obsidian mirrors for scrying, as an alternative to the more common quartz crystal ball. Obsidian amulets are also used to reflect away harmful psychic influences. Similarly, opal protects the whole body against magical attack. The gentle greenish gem peridot is used to counter disorders of the digestive system and to bring balance to the mind.

Quartz, or rock crystal, is the most familiar of all magical crystals. Balls made from quartz are favored for scrying, while quartz crystals protect the dead from demonic attack. Magically, and in healing, it has the power to clear blockages. (For further details about the other magical qualities of quartz, see chapter 2). Ruby's blood-red color gives a sympathetic link with the blood. Rubies guard magically against blood loss. Crystal magicians use them to treat all kinds of disorders of the blood.

Generally, sapphire is used to suppress obsession with the self, bringing calmness to agitated people. Sapphires occur in different colors. Star sapphires are best when we need the power of calming. Pinkish-violet and orange sapphires are said to promote selfless love. Cornflower blue sapphires are said to prolong youthfulness and promote longevity. Dark-blue sapphires are used to treat fever and nervous illnesses. Worn together with pinkish-violet stones, a dark-blue sapphire brings the wearer a more humane attitude to life.

Topaz is used to counter nervous disorders and insomnia. It is valuable as a psychic barrier against magical attack and as an amulet against sudden death. Tourmaline is reputed to be an all-healing gemstone, while turquoise assists us in summoning helpful spiritual powers.

Fig. C.I. Wheel of the Powers

A Valid
and Appropriate
Spiritual Path

We live in a time of perpetual and accelerating change. Traditional ways of doing things are rapidly breaking down in the face of globalization. The destruction of nature by the products of industry is happening all around us. It is self-evident that unless we develop a better attitude toward nature, we will bring about our own ruin. Recognizing this, many people are seeking a better way of living. This has brought about a rediscovery and popularization of techniques that once were known by very few people.

In former times, techniques of natural spirituality were handed down by word of mouth within families and from teacher to student. Occasionally, they appeared in handwritten texts or small-circulation books. Today, all of this has changed. Communion with nature through trees, animals, stones, and landscape features, once discouraged by those in authority, is no longer to be hidden. In the past, this spiritual tradition survived because it adapted itself continuously to new conditions as they arose.

In a continually changing and developing world, natural magic cannot stand still. We cannot make believe that we are living in a primal world of primitive purity—even if that ever existed. Neither should we complain that the modern world is not what it was in former times. For better or for worse, we are alive here and now, and we must live and operate under the given conditions. Society has developed, responding to new conditions of life as they arose. Today, natural spirituality also continues to adapt to new conditions. It has reclaimed its rightful position as a valid and appropriate spiritual path, an antidote to the gross materialism of much of modernity. It gives us a unique means to discover and create harmony and beauty in our lives.

FINIS

Index

Page numbers in *italics* indicate illustrations.